A
CABINETMAKER'S
NOTEBOOK

A

CABINET

NOTE

JAMES KRENOV

MAKER'S

BOOK

VAN NOSTRAND REINHOLD COMPANY
NEW YORK CINCINNATI TORONTO LONDON MELBOURNE

But they [craftsmen] keep stable the fabric of the world,
and their prayer is in the practice of their trade.

SIRACH 38:34

COPYRIGHT © 1976 BY LITTON EDUCATIONAL PUBLISHING, INC.
Library of Congress Catalog Card Number 75-30233
ISBN 0-442-24551-3

Published in 1976 by Van Nostrand Reinhold Company
A Division of Litton Educational Publishing, Inc.
135 West 50th Street, New York, N.Y. 10020

Van Nostrand Reinhold Limited
1410 Birchmount Road
Scarborough, Ontario M1P 2E7, Canada

Van Nostrand Reinhold Australia Pty. Ltd.
17 Queen Street
Mitcham, Victoria 3132, Australia

Van Nostrand Reinhold Company Ltd.
Molly Millars Lane
Wokingham, Berkshire, England

BOOK DESIGN BY JEAN CALLAN KING/VISUALITY

Library of Congress Cataloging in Publication Data

Krenov, James.
  A cabinetmaker's notebook.

  Includes index.
  1. Krenov, James. 2. Cabinet-work. I. Title.
TT140.K73A33   684.1'04'0924 [B]   75-30233
ISBN 0-442-24551-3

Acknowledgments

In order to write about one's craft, one needs first to survive as a craftsman. So if the many persons who through the years have shown their appreciation must here be nameless, they are not forgotten.

As to this book: Craig McArt, now at the Rochester Institute of Technology, was one of the first to urge me to start. George Brady and Robert H. Johnston, also at RIT, prodded me further. From Sheridan College in Canada, Donald L. McKinley contributed humor and provocative questions.

In Sweden, where lately craftsmen going against the current tend to evoke frowns, there has been encouragement too: Algot Törneman at the Swedish Royal Academy of Arts, Dag Widman of the National Museum, John Sjöström, Professor, Pär Frank at Natur o Kultur—these are but a few of those who through all kinds of weather have been a real help.

A word of gratitude must also go to all those who opened their homes to photographer Bengt Carlèn and his sensitive camera.

Finally, a humble but lasting thanks to my students, wherever they may be, whose energy and enthusiasm carried me along when my own were not enough.

James Krenov

PHOTOGRAPHS BY BENGT CARLÈN, STOCKHOLM

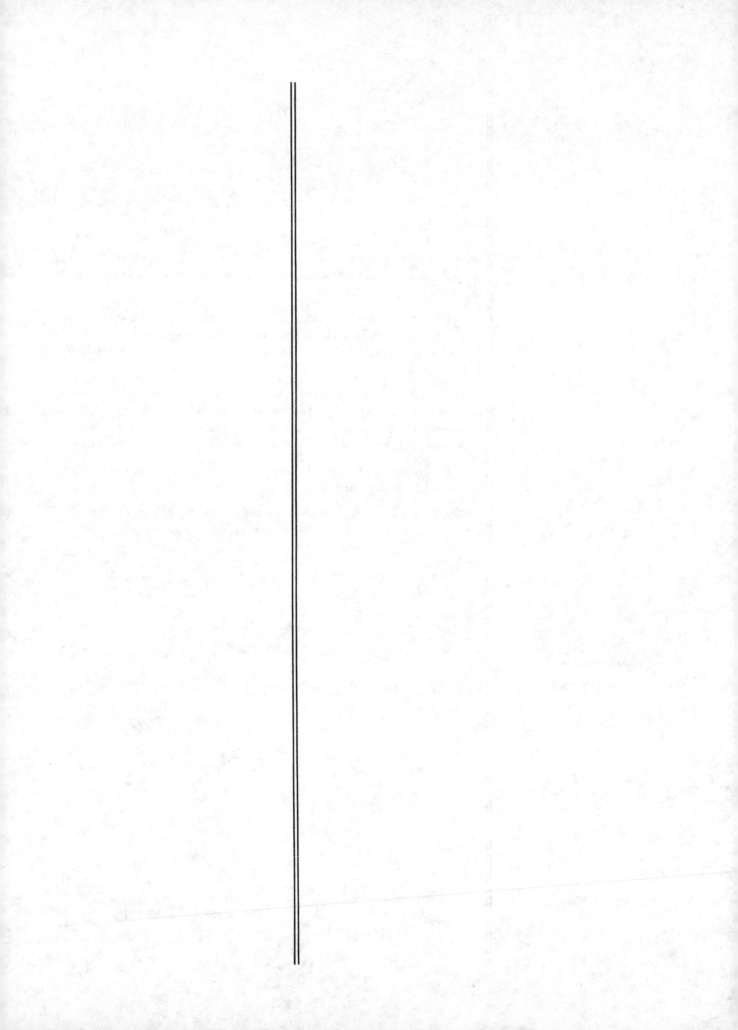

THE WOODCARVER

Khing, the master carver, made a bell stand
Of precious wood. When it was finished,
All who saw it were astounded. They said it must be
The work of spirits.
The Prince of Lu said to the master carver:
"What is your secret?"

Khing replied: "I am only a workman:
I have no secret. There is only this:
When I began to think about the work you commanded
I guarded my spirit, did not expend it
On trifles, that were not to the point.
I fasted in order to set
My heart at rest.
After three days fasting,
I had forgotten gain and success.
After five days
I had forgotten praise or criticism.
After seven days
I had forgotten my body
with all its limbs.

"By this time all thought of your Highness
And of the court had faded away.
All that might distract me from the work
Had vanished.
I was collected in the single thought
Of the bell stand.

"Then I went to the forest
To see the trees in their own natural state.
When the right tree appeared before my eyes,
The bell stand also appeared in it, clearly, beyond doubt.
All I had to do was to put forth my hand.
And begin.

"If I had not met this particular tree,
There would have been
No bell stand at all.

"What happened?
My own collected thought
Encountered the hidden potential in the wood;
From this live encounter came the work
Which you ascribe to the spirits."

From THE WAY OF CHUANG TZU by Thomas Merton
Copyright © 1965 by the Abbey of Gethsemani.
New Directions Publishing Corporation.

7

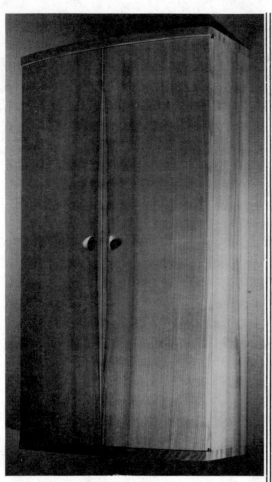

Cabinet in Swedish yellow ash. The softness of form is due to the play of the wood, which, besides the graphic lines of the grain, has its own soft texture. Height 85 cm., width 46 cm., depth 16 cm. Untreated. 1970.

IT'S ALWAYS A LITTLE DIFFICULT FOR ME TO BEGIN

talking about wood because it is usually a matter of looking at it in one of two ways. One way is a generality, as just a material that we make things of—and that for me, is too wide, shallow, and impersonal. But there are people for whom wood and working with wood is not simply a profession but a very intimate thing: the relationship between the person and the material, and *how* they are doing it. I mean how they are doing it in the most intimate detailed sense; the relationship between wood and the tools that they use, between their feelings, their intuitions, and their dreams. Wood, considered that way, is to me *alive*.

I always think of wood as being alive. I grew up in primitive places, in the North where there were many legends and the supposition that some objects were animated and alive with a spirit of their own. Sometimes, when I work, this creeps into the atmosphere: the sense that maybe the wood and the tools are doing, and want to do, something which is beyond me, a part of me, but more than I am. And I don't want to ask too many questions about this. I note it as a curiosity, perhaps a bit exaggerated, but there is always this element of discovery, the sense of something happening which is more than you expect.

Wood, thought of that way, very personal and elusive, is almost a way of living. Various people have asked me about this, and in talking about it one or another would say, "You know, you have a love affair with wood." Perhaps this is true; it is a kind of lifelong love affair with wood and everything that is around it.

About seventeen or eighteen years ago, when I first began looking around for wood, we had in Stockholm at least one little yard, one of those family places—a couple of brothers with a very, very small stock; odds and ends of wood. Such yards are gone now. They were out of date then. Those brothers (Forsberg was their name) were still living in the spirit of the time when there were old-time cabinetmakers around, doing inlay work and piecework of their own, and interested in all these woods, which really used to be traditional cabinetmakers' woods, and one could just presume that they were available. Many old pieces of furniture have the drawers made out of doussie because it is easy to work, very stable, and it doesn't warp. So they had doussie, odds and ends of this and that. Somebody would come to them and say, "I've cut down two chestnut trees," and they knew where there was a sawmill, one of those small, one-man sawmills, and they'd cut up this chestnut log or two or maybe even three or four.

The maple that was coming from the Continent then was all white, just like the ash is almost white. But the Swedish maple was like a tree that I saw in Boston one day that had fallen over on Bay State Road. It had begun to deteriorate near the ground and then during a storm that day, it fell over. There was an awful lot of gorgeous color coming up though that tree, just absolutely gorgeous. Well, these brothers would get a log like that and they would saw it up and there were still one or two odd chaps around who would come and buy a plank or two. You could turn half the pile or the whole pile and just look at all these pieces. Nobody would say to you, "There's the five hundred feet, a great big stack, and we'll take what the fork truck can reach, right off the top. If you don't like it that way—go somewhere else." They didn't say that. They were interested not just in the business, but also in the kind of people who cared about the material they were handling, and were almost grateful there was still somebody around appreciating it and working with it. I started going there. I had a very, very tiny shop, just a band saw, not even a jointer.

So I was working this way, from day to day, living on less than a shoestring; I could hardly buy a shoestring. Sometimes I saw a log that I should have bought but couldn't afford. They let me buy one plank and I was sorry ever after that I couldn't buy the whole log because soon it was gone; this was the last of it, ever. And the last of the old-fashioned one-man companies, the romantic attitudes, the impractical approach; everything.

I don't think that I started out fascinated by the variety within one particular kind of wood. I wasn't experienced enough; what really fascinated me was variety of woods: there were still ten or fifteen kinds of exotic woods there at Forsbergs. I jumped from doussie to bubinga to something else to something still better. It was only years later that I began to rediscover the richness within certain woods. It gradually got to me that maple as a wood is infinitely rich. When I started out, I wasn't aware of that. At school we talk about American woods and say it is quite possible to limit oneself to wood from one region or even from one state, and that's absolutely right. Wharton Esherik said that if you can't

Sawing Tasmanian blackwood. Once sent from its native forest to London, where I found it under some twenty years' worth of dust and grime.

find the wood you need around your own backyard, there is no sense in being a woodworker. He did most of his work with the wood he found near the place where he lived in Philadelphia. I quite agree and accept that, but then I disagree. A painter can spend his whole life painting one motif, you know; his entire life of painting is really just variations on a theme—Toulouse-Lautrec with his cafes, Degas with his dancers. And it is enough, wonderful. On the other hand, some painters spent years painting one motif and then suddenly made a journey to another country, or something happened in their life, and from then on, you can see, they painted differently. Whether better or worse we won't go into, but certainly there was a change in their way of seeing things. Maybe instead of just one theme, they were painting many different themes in many quite different ways.

Now I see the fascination of each log of maple—every one is sort of a curiosity and different from the next—but at the same time, in addition to maple, I like knowing that I can get hold of other woods, not because they are better, but different: another mood, still another way of working. Maybe there is a little romantic story behind it. For example, this wood—somebody sent it to me from São Paulo in Brazil and they sent it, all 1,900 pounds, as samples for Señor Krenov in Stockholm. Or I find now and then a scrap somewhere that someone has had for years and years and years; maybe he's a sculptor and he's dead, or he's very, very old and won't work anymore, so he turns it over to a yard and says, "Sell it," and they don't even know the name of the wood. They sold me a billet of cocobolo as rosewood. I didn't know any better and they didn't know any better. When I opened it up, I realized it was cocobolo, and it was a tremendous experience. Like finding a precious stone in a sand pit. So now I think it's a combination of being aware of the fact that there are tremendous variations within any particular kind of wood. Well—most woods: we won't say there's all that much variation in some. But in most woods there is a fair variation. In addition to that, when you can get something from far off, something that is hard to get and quite, quite different, it gives you an emotional experience. You go around being happy. And worried too. You think, "I've only got these two planks. What am I going to make? What am I going to make out of these two planks? It should take the two planks—almost—I still have to have a little bit of margin in case I spoil something,

An "opened" half-log of Andaman padouk, rich
reddish-orange wood. A rarity nowadays.

in case something goes wrong. So I had better not play it too
close. Still, I want to make it out of this wood." This becomes
a challenge. It is quite an adventure really. It can be pretty
hair-raising, because you know that if you muff it, that's it:
you can't get on the phone and say, "Look, I just spoiled one
piece of plank—send me another," and go over and pick up
another plank. The answer on the telephone is "Ha, ha, ha!"

So that's the way it is. Those days are gone, at least in most
places, though not everywhere. Even without romance, there
are those who deal with wood because they like it. Thus, I
have now a good relationship with a hardwood company in
Stockholm which can supply me with flitch-cut logs (not,
as is often the case, random-sawn to get the most commercial
value out of the log). The foremen there are rather amused
by this fellow who still insists on picking and poking and
prying his way through the yard, nagging them until they get
the right wood. Every year I am after them, calling them up
to ask for more. "Have you sawn a log of maple yet?" "No."
"Well, then, try to find me an old straight maple—old maples
have the dark colors likely to be present in the heart. And
get me a Swedish ash. How about elms?" We don't have the
elm blight in Sweden, so they cut an elm now and then. Occa-
sionally they will call me up unexpectedly and say, "We have
this log—just one, for you. How shall we saw it?" And I will
say, "Cut it two inches, but leave a big four inch plank through
the heart." (We are talking about flitch-cutting: they understand that). And they will do this for me, and will even store
the wood at their place for a year, maybe two. There is a stand-
ing joke around the yard about Krenov's pile of lumber, although they are extremely kind and generous. They will allow
me to go and look and even ask them to deliver a few planks of
a certain log to me.

That, really, is the beginning; the fact that we have access
to wood in relation to logs. Related planks between which
we can see a purpose.

One could do it in America. I know very well that in some
places this sort of thing is possible, although I doubt that it's
being done seriously. It will come, though. There is a hesitancy,
something lacking in the crafts climate as yet, to make this
become important enough for people to persevere.

After the wood is sawn and lies around air-drying at the
yard, it comes to my little shop. There are some stairs to go
down and some turns to make, which is difficult, but I get

11

Getting wood down the stairs.

these planks inside the shop, and I live with them. They are all around me; I'm alone with them, and we get to know each other through the years. Some of them become like an old friend, or maybe an enemy, because I have moved hundreds of pounds of wood many times just to take another look at them. Sometimes they match up with an idea I have, or a wish that someone has expressed. So these planks come to be woven into my existence and into my plans, and then things grow from these pieces of wood I have.

A craftsman's work is heavy work. People come and say, "Well, here you are. How does it feel to be an artist, to be doing artist's work?" Now that's naive, because I spend long hours moving these heavy planks all alone, working in the machine room where the dust is so thick I can hardly see the walls, and the noise is pounding. And maybe I'll have to work three or four days with very great discipline and concentration to get to the stage where, later on, when the wood goes through still another period of drying, I can finally do the fine, sensitive side of the work. But first I have to discipline myself to do this other work, which involves hard labor and concentration of another sort, often forgotten, because this kind of wood crafting is a combination of many things; discipline, a strong back, intuition, skilled fingers, something in the eye, and something more than professional skill—perhaps someone else can explain it better than I.

My way of working is just a long series of personal discoveries. I can't give anyone secrets, something that I promise will work, because, finally, it depends upon one's skill and intuition, and other things. But I can give hints, the benefit of some experience in the things that have happened to me. I don't get kiln-dried wood because I think that kiln-dried wood has been killed. This is not a pun, but a fact. The process of saturating wood with steam and getting it all wet, cooking it, you might say, is a chemical process that changes and dulls the color of the wood, and the fibers are affected so that wood which has been kiln-dried feels different to me. It's got a different ring, a different texture; it isn't clear and fine. It's like a poorly developed photograph—one that was taken well but just didn't come out. Besides, kiln-dried wood is brittle.

Many people don't realize these truths because they have never been close enough to real wood, beautiful wood in its natural state. They've seen veneered surfaces; they've lived with wood secondhand, and they are just not aware

12

of the richness that is to be found in individual pieces, logs and planks. So part of my struggle through the years, both with visitors to my shop and in some of my brief writing, has been to try to remind people of these things, to tell them not only about the richness of the material, but the connection between the material and how some few people, a very few people, work. In a way, I can prepare them to receive these objects, or meet these objects, and expose themselves to them with a degree of sensitivity which the objects, I hope, deserve.

This is truly an unexplored chapter in the United States. Expression in wood, if I may say so, is a bit heavy-handed there; oversimplified. So often the emphasis is on form— as in sculpture. It is primarily a visual experience, with the wood not always having its say, not always as important as it should be—sometimes not important at all. Some artists in wood order their material by telephone, and admit that it is not of that great importance. This is not a criticism; it is merely stating that there are different relationships to the material. But when it is important, then the difference between kiln-dried wood and natural, fine, unspoiled wood such as I have is great, and that affects me emotionally. It gives me a sense of richness. I feel it differently under my cutting tools, my planes, my chisels. It's different in the surfaces that I bring out, in the way that I treat it finally, or do not treat it. Many of the things I make are not treated in any way afterwards, because nothing that I can put on them will enhance the beauty of the natural wood. Sometimes, of course, wood needs to be treated for a particular usage; a wood like doussie, which comes from Africa, makes a beautiful table top and it takes oil wonderfully. It acquires a rich, reddish brown color, and the oiled surface is quite insensitive to abuse. You can spill almost anything on it, and touch it up with a bit of oil and steel wool. It is then as good as ever; in fact, it gets better through the years.

We come to the matter of judging the condition that wood is in: the dryness. You know, I live with my wood a long time and still, very seldom are the planks that I go into really dry. So I have developed a way of working with them in stages. I presaw them, perhaps while I'm working on something else, and for days or weeks or months they dry completely. And during that time, I observe them. I know how they finally will be when they are dry, and I allow for changes that are

Unloading wood from the truck.

going to take place. This approach is, in a way, wasteful, but, on the other hand, it is the only way to work with wood which is not completely dry when you get it; to get on good personal terms with it.

So we talk about tools, we talk about objects, and I hope that gradually I can get across this relationship, this love affair or whatever you will. How it comes to be that woods whisper to you about tools and methods and shapes—shapes within shapes, really, because when you become aware of certain ways of using wood, then you realize something about a straight line. To me there is no real life in a perfectly straight line or a perfect circle. But in wood you can make a rectangular object, give it tension and countertension and balance without complete symmetry, and you can give it rhythm by choosing the wood. You may have just a rectangular frame, but you can make it almost soft, almost a sensation of oval for the eye, if you choose the wood in the right way. And you can do the opposite; make it unpleasant by having the wood bow slightly upward and inward so that the corners appear extremely sharp to the eye; this will be disturbing, whereas the other is harmonious. But it is not dead, or lax, because wood is a living material when used in this way. You are always experimenting. You are playing with textures, tensions, the things that happen, and, if you are sensitive, if you are lucky enough, then you may exceed your expectations. I've never believed that you have to be all that inventive. Form, for me, is not the primary thing, form is only a beginning. It is the combination of feelings and a function; shapes and things that come to one in connection with the discoveries made as one goes into the wood that pull it all together and give meaning to form.

So, mostly, I believe in the fact that I will be able to combine all this, to make an object that is simple, practical and pleasing. A small wall cabinet which you put things in, or leave empty if you wish, you have it as something to give you harmony or excitement of some kind, an experience, just as painting or sculpture does. Sometimes the objects I make border on the nonfunctional, the function being of secondary importance; but I like very much to work where the function is rather direct, and the pieces are going to be useful. I like a beautifully made drawer with its own whisper and its light movement and the fact that you can take it all the way out if you have guests at home or if you just want to do so. You pull it all the way out, and you look at the back of it, and you see that someone has really cared. The back is as fine as the front. The bottom isn't plywood; there is no part that makes you say, "Well, don't look at this; it's not important, it's at the back of the thing, you know, and you never really see it."

Working alone poses problems of discipline and aims, and you have to get on lifelong terms with your work and yourself. For most of us, in the beginning stages and perhaps always, it's a condition of struggle and discovery and secret satisfactions. Sometimes you are not making as much money as the plumber or the pipefitter, but you are alive with your work, and I think that one of the important points to keep you going is that you enjoy it—not hobby enjoyment or periodic enjoyment, but the enjoyment of *being* with it. That, of course, means that you must save your energy, you must develop methods of working with wood that lead to a sort of harmony, a satisfaction that you are, with a minimum of effort, achieving the maximum of sensitivity. You are saying what you want to say, finally, and you're doing it in a way that, despite all the sweat and hard work, gives you satisfaction. This is the way you want to live.

Of course, one of the great troubles has been that people have not always understood that this kind of craftsman usually does fine, honest work—work that will last a long time and be fine to experience. And the craftsman—a vicious circle—the craftsman gradually becomes alarmed and saddened, and even humiliated by his inability to make ends meet. At that point something happens to all but a very few. Things change somehow. A small compromise leads to another small compromise, and finally we wind up doing something that we do not really love. It's a sneaky thing.

I think that what I would like to do before it is too late is to get this across to a few craftsmen-to-be who will work after me, and also to a public which will be there to receive them, because we are living in a time when, I believe, this is important. Fine things in wood are important, not only aesthetically, as oddities or rarities, but because we are becoming aware of the fact that much of our life is spent buying and discarding, and buying again, things that are not good. Some of us long to have at least something, somewhere, which will give us harmony and a sense of durability—I won't say permanence, but durability—things that, through the years, become more and more beautiful, things we can leave to our children. We

Above: *Much of the blackwood being sawed has cracked through the years; only part of it will finally be usable. But that part is hard, fine to work— beautiful. (See cabinet, page 121.)*
Below: *Unloading.*

can enjoy them while we are here, and even if we can't surround ourselves with these things (we can't, of course, and we shouldn't), they should be here for those of us who long for this sort of thing.

I've never believed that a really good craftsman is intended for a tremendous public. A museum can show a thing or two to countless people, but the craftsman lives in a condition where the size of his public is almost in inverse porportion to the quality of his work. It sounds like a contradiction, but what I mean by quality is the total content of the work that he does. And he really hasn't that much use for a hundred or two hundred people each year banging on his door, wanting things, because, finally, this craftsman is the one who does the work himself, and gives people something very personal, not very much of it, but very personal and therefore not accessible to everyone.

To the right people it brings joy, and I think that if some of this form of craft were handled better by educators and museums, people who want to help the crafts, then even more craftsmen would be encouraged to try to become aware of wood in this sense, and become attuned to wood. Wood with luster, with depth of tone, with delicacy; coarseness— masculine woods, feminine woods. It's a matter of mood and method, and the whole thing then becomes a cycle and a way of working, with wood as the beginning of it all.

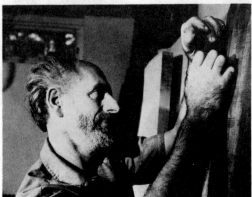

Above: *Sorting, re-sorting, looking for the beginning of something. Some of these planks have been with me for seven or more years.*

Left: *Planing maple for a closer look at the true color under the rough-sawn surface.*

Right: *Carrying and carrying again is a part of everyday life.*
Below: *A first guess—and an exploratory cut. A fine bandsaw is indispensable.*

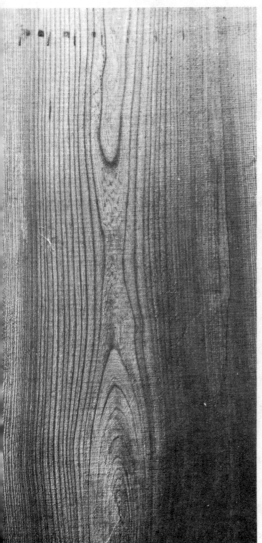

Hopes, surprises—and disappointments. This piece of elm looked fine at first; the other side showed a pit and deep crack: the beautiful arch pattern was unusable.

Round table in Rio rosewood. The flare of the legs is hand-planed, the bevel done with spokeshave and file. The positioning of the legs came first, and determined the size of the top. Diameter 48 cm., height 59 cm. Waxed. 1968.

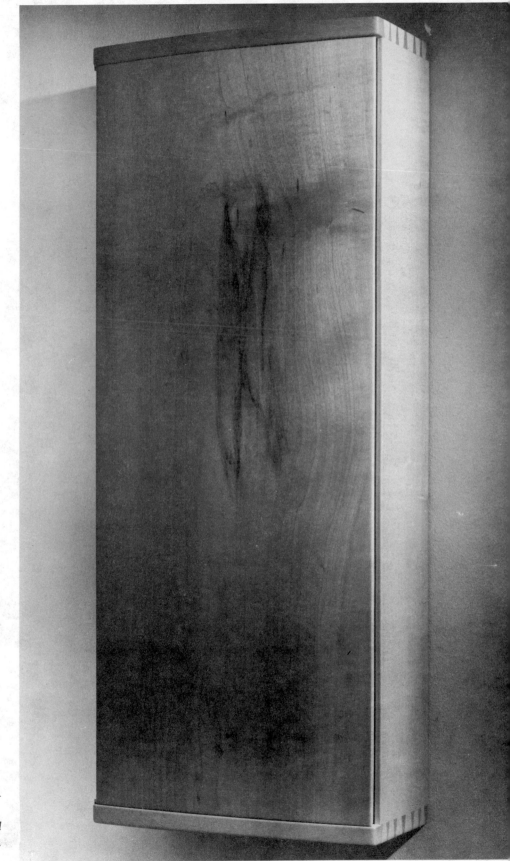

Cabinet in maple, one of my favorite woods. The detail shows the pattern, the last thin part outside the heartwood. A few more flattening cuts, and it would be lost. Height 74 cm., width 31 cm., depth 14 cm. Waxed.

Floor cabinet-showcase in lemonwood, and details. A difficult piece, never re-peated, it has a fine home. Height 160 cm., width 67 cm., maximum depth 23 cm. The outside is oil-finished. 1967.

THERE HAS ALWAYS BEEN SOMETHING OF AN IN-
consistency in our approach to functional things in wood. This
is a biased statement, yes. But imagine it now as a combination of several factors.

There is the attitude, all too prevalent in the crafts, that any
kind of work will do when the wood is really exotic stuff. You
can do mediocre work and still people want it. They will
say, "Look at that *wood!*"

Then again, wood is so common—we have everyday things
in wood all around us constantly—quite lifeless. These are
products of industry and they are necessary; they are part of
our environment. Yet they do build a curtain between us
and the true possibilities of the material and its values. They
keep us from seeing the practical possibilities, as well as the
aesthetic ones. These everyday market products are wood,
yes, but they lack any humility toward the material, or respect,
or even simple practical consideration. Because most often
they are very poorly designed, poorly put together, created and
accepted more out of habit than awareness. They simply do
not last.

We go and we search for something for our homes, find
what we think we want. Pay a fair price for it, take it home. And
then watch it become soiled and dingy, dry and scuffed, too
soon overused. Maybe we pay the junk man to come and get it,
or we take it to the scrap heap. Then we start all over again.
Go to the stores, search, buy again. And again it's just paper-
thin veneer and lacquered surfaces, bad construction and
imitation style. (I don't know why, but the aspect of imitation,
of having something which we can recognize in another
image, is almost a compulsion these days. We have to identify
every object with something else, even if it is called "original."
Yet, however far back we go, we will encounter imitation:
American colonial furniture, after all, was in a sense an
imitation.)

The buying of this kind of furniture does not make sense,
aesthetically or even economically. Over a period of ten years
one person may buy, let us say, three or four coffee tables, each
one probably costing more than the last. This person does
not object to the cost, a market price on each table. He will buy,
wear, and throw away, and then go and look for the next and
the next. Now suppose we make this same citizen a table out of
solid doussie wood that is oil-finished and will last for fifty

years or more and grow beautiful as it is being used; that will give off a quality sound when a glass or cup is placed on it. This table costs no more than do any two factory-made tables. What? The person in question says, "It's outrageous!" Of late I have been trying to ask the question as firmly as I can, "Outrageous on what basis; in relation to what?"

We are becoming environmentally conscious. We're aware of certain experiences. We like to touch each other, and profess to have a renewed sensual content in our living. We talk about all these emotions of ours, these wonderful new feelings. All right. Then let us put some of these emotions and values to work in the surroundings most close to us. Let's be consistent. You buy a piece of jewelry for your girl or your wife or whomever, and it's *supposed* to cost. If it is inexpensive, it's junk. She won't have it. *There* we can be consistent. We allow it to cost. In fact we boast about the fact that it did cost. We could, at least on a small scale, apply this principle to some of the practical objects around us.

There is nothing new in this. Others have said it before and said it much better. But what has consistently encouraged me, and I in turn have tried to get it across to other people, is that the only principle justifying the existence of a certain kind of craftsman is that we can give people things which these other sources with their equipment, Mr. Timesaver and Mr. Designer and Mr. Artie Craftsman, can not give them.

I don't know how one defines the word "quality" in wood. But I believe there is a measure that will hold *both* aesthetically and practically. All my life as a craftsman I have been trying, often in vain, to prove this point. The final challenge is that aesthetics and function do go beautifully together. More craftsmen should be working in a way where this shows in the things we do. Trying to achieve this very elusive goal is *the* challenge. No doubt this point will never be proved, partly because in America there is a national idiom and a cultural level which are working against people, even the sensitive ones, being aware of what the integrity of wood really means. There just hasn't been enough of that kind of work around lately. We hardly have a contemporary scale of measure here, other than recognizably reassuring or way-out new. This sad truth is easier to reject than to disprove. Certain aspects in the way of life of a country are, by their very nature, *for* refinement in some crafts, and against others. Subtle factors of thorough-

Opposite: *Wall cabinet in Swedish fir, drawers of cherry wood. Coopered door with surface hand-planed. Top and bottom profiles carved to shape. This cabinet was mostly a result of having made fine wooden planes. Height 57 cm., width 32 cm., depth 16 cm. First made in 1957.*
Above: *Detail of the side. A corresponding groove just behind the other side of the door provides a finger-hold for opening it.*

ness, patience, and humility are at a disadvantage; whereas other purely visual aspects have an easier time in this particular climate.

Still, when I teach in America I find myself forgetting this and being more hopeful than I should be. Because the young people are wonderful and spontaneous and enthusiastic, and some of them very sensitive, I find myself encouraging them and trying even to imagine what it would be like if educators and publishers and other people could provide even a small and select public with the information, the awareness and the emotional preparation that is necessary to respond to their future work at its best. I imagine this can be done. Sometimes it almost feels as though it is just around the corner; that someone should try, and receive help, so we can provide a better reception for these people with the sensitivity towards the material and the patience to develop their skills and the intuition to provide a message of their own.

Then somehow, during the process of hoping, I meet again and again the institutional problems, the deceptive educational-political aspects. Maybe things aren't all that bad and I have just been unlucky. But too often there really is ignorance concerning the final goal—something so vague as "fine crafts," or "excellence"—ignorance of what can be achieved by a few and how it can be used to encourage and enrich the many. Amid maneuvering, the *usability* of the best crafts is muddled, and lost.

Education assumes (in order to justify itself to trustees and public) the role of being both selective and "democratic." This is often disastrous, and results in work on a level of generalities.

The best is by its very nature selective: why not accept it as such? This doesn't make crafts as nostalgia or entertainment or therapy less justifiable. It's simply that as a dedication, as the center of one's life, craft is one thing—and as anything else it is a different and separate matter.

Both are needed. Between them we should have an enriching dialogue. But force them together and you get gibberish.

What to do, where to start? I dare not be optimistic. Perhaps schools, however well meaning, cannot give us the answer. As it is, there will certainly be compromises and opportunism, at the expense of those who are most vulnerable, who could share with us some of the experiences we profess to want so much—if only we would give them the chance.

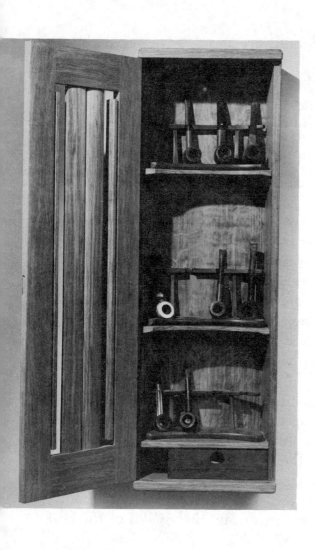

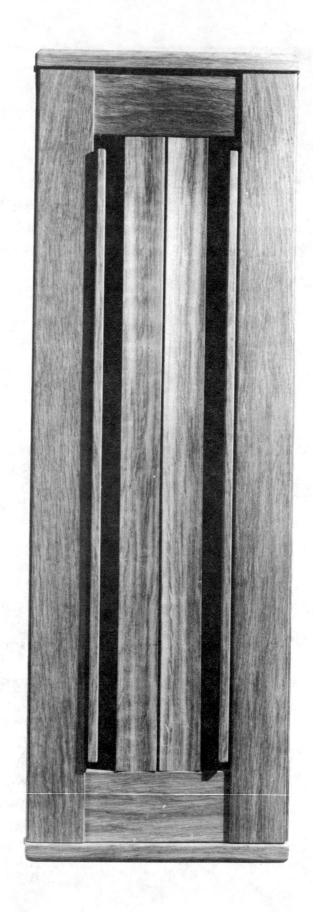

Pipe cabinet in English brown oak. The problem was to combine a pleasing shape with ventilation for the much-used pipes inside. A pipe-smoker is often a putterer with his pipes: the stands inside are removable. The box is for cleaners, etc. Height 86 cm., width 26 cm., depth 14 cm. Untreated. 1968.

28

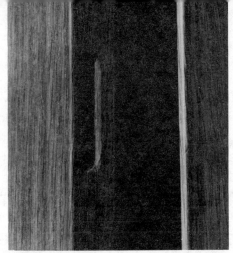

Details of pipe cabinet: grip at right-hand edge of door (left) and closeup of the door. The middle pieces of the door are hand-planed into a slight hollow.

"Tuning" a favorite plane. My planes are as sensitive as fine musical instruments.

A LONG TIME AGO, I SPENT SOME TIME IN A SCHOOL for cabinetmakers in Sweden. It was a good school, and had fairly good tools. I remember the old-fashioned Danish wooden planes there, which were rather awkward but had fairly good cutting properties. And I recall a book in the office about old Norwegian tools—a quaint history of the plane. It was about excavations that had turned up the tools with which the Oseberg Viking ship was made hundreds of years ago. Then, too, our teacher used to tell us about the old-timers and how they made their own tools, planes among them, and I began to think of the plane as being the cabinetmaker's violin; the instrument that sets the tone of the music in an orchestra. For me, now, it is *the* tool, in the sense that I enjoy planing the wood with a true plane more perhaps than any other aspect of working. Well, I like also to carve with a knife, and I enjoy working with sharp chisels or a nicely shaped spokeshave, but planing is something special—like the music of the violin.

When I think about a plane, I am thinking about the fine points. That is, how well it is made, how much work it will do for you, and how much enjoyment it will give. I know very well that a boatbuilder or a carpenter doing very large, rough work needn't be affected by this because the final sensitivity that I am talking about in planes is for the person who wants them and needs them and will appreciate them when doing smallish, sensitive things. I make my own planes—of fine wood and fine steel—not out of nostalgia for bygone days, but because I think that if you have the finest planes, if you have succeeded in making yourself some really fine tools, it does prompt you to work more carefully. Such tools spare energy, they save time for you, and I believe that they allow you to work more joyfully to exceed the performances that you have done before.

At a store for woodworker's tools in America, I saw antique tools, mostly planes, made of exotic woods. As objects they were quite charming—a charm that cost seventy or eighty dollars, and might be worth it. After all, those were the days, and we are becoming more and more curious about them. Old tools, old houses, old anything—we are looking for something lost. There are things to be found, there is knowledge to be gained. The question is: how do you use that knowledge to go ahead, not just back? My friend Captain Coffin told me about clipper ships and working sails. Thrilled, I wanted to sail.

But I had to learn about nylon sails and flexible rigs before I could race a star boat.

To the antique tools again. The very parts of those planes which were most important to their cutting properties— the opening for the iron, the shape and finish of the breaker— these parts were simply not designed to do the sensitive work we are talking about. They won't do the job—not because they are old and worn down—though that may be a part of it— but because they were put together as tools, not with the final element of discovery that would make them into an *instrument*. After all, there was no need to do so. Life then was different, people made things another way, under other conditions, for other and more obvious purposes.

Well, for me the discovery at the school was a turning point. It meant a lot to me; it may have been what set me on my present course. At that time I didn't know anything about the future. I wasn't even sure that I wanted to continue with cabinetmaking. I had grown up with boats and wood, true, but I was just groping. I think, looking back at it now, this was the point at which I began to really enjoy the tactile aspect of wood. Surfaces began to appear and I discovered things. I remember the fellows around me who would come to look at the shavings out of curiosity, and they would look at the surfaces, stand around talking about them, and later on one or two of them made planes for themselves, I think. But they were really aware of the fact that here was something that was a bit extra.

There are also practical advantages to these little tools, because this kind of plane is one that you can hold in many different ways in your hand. You can hold it in one hand and plane an edge. You can put your whole hand over it, and when you have very rough-grained wood you can make circular motions the way you do sometimes to get a flat surface. And a really fine plane will cut truly sharp with the breaker and the iron just right. In the sense that I mean it, such a plane will do small wonders for you. I don't know if I can prove that. One has to get to the point of discovery by trying in order to begin to see how these things add up, and if it's the right thing for you, then it might mean a great deal later on.

This is just a basic idea of what planes mean to me, and a reminder of the fact that it is a bit of work, worth it only if you expect certain good results and are willing to be patient about it. Because people may say, "Well, he's the guy who uses wooden planes, but his work isn't the better for it." That would be rather sad to hear, but I think that when you've made them a while, and when you are patient enough and sensitive enough, the best wooden planes will improve your work and your enjoyment of the work too.

I can join two pieces of maple, a little bit coopered or at some angle, and join them so beautifully that I don't have to force them together. They almost want to be together. I just put a little pressure on them, and have a nice tight joint with no glue showing in the white wood. It's that tight.

People come to me and say, "Oh, you're the fellow that planes everything." That, of course, is ridiculous because many woods aren't intended to be planed, and I don't plane these, but some of the results that I achieve are due to my planes, and go back to that discovery I made with the first one.

I stand at my workbench. Shavings curl from the plane in my hands, swish-and-slide, as I rock to the motion of work. The smell of fresh-cut wood, a slick, silvery yellow surface gleaming under the tireless plane, and a feeling of contentment. Nothing is wrong. Here am I, here is my work—and someone is waiting for the fruits of these fleeting hours. My contentment is bound by the whitewashed walls of my little cellar shop, by the stacks of long-sought woods with their mild colors and elusive smells, by the planked ceiling through which I hear the quick footsteps of a child—and yet it is boundless, my joy. The cabinet is taking shape. Someone is waiting for it. With a bit of luck, it will be liked, given continuity in a life of its own. Hands will caress this shimmery surface, a thumb will discover the edge which I am rounding. An edge rounded with my plane. An edge cut rounded, but not sandpapered—a sensitive finger will understand its living imperfections and be pleased at the traces left by sharp steel on hardwood. Through the years this edge will be polished, change tone, gleam in mellowness. Yet always it will bear the marks of my favorite tool.

Right: *Planing concave door, English brown oak cabinet.*

Below: *Only a part of making a wooden plane worth the effort.*

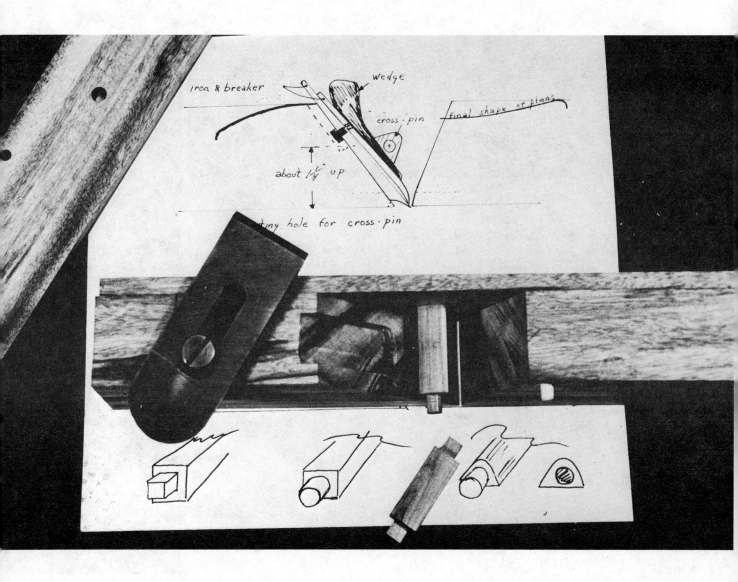

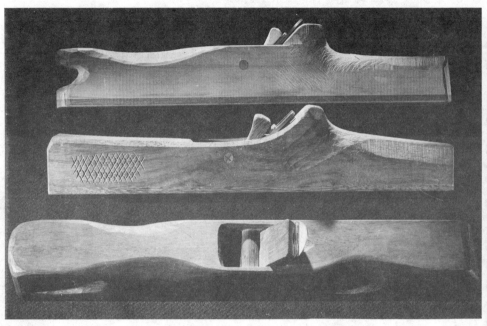

Above: *A few old favorites. From top to bottom: an early plane of boxwood; one of Indian laurel; the third of Andaman padouk, made in 1960 and unequaled in its performance for me. Length 47 cm.*
Opposite, top: *Honing plane irons. There is a difference between the concept of sharpness and a truly sharp tool.*
Right: *Polishing-plane of cocobolo. Compact, easy in the hand, a joy to use.*

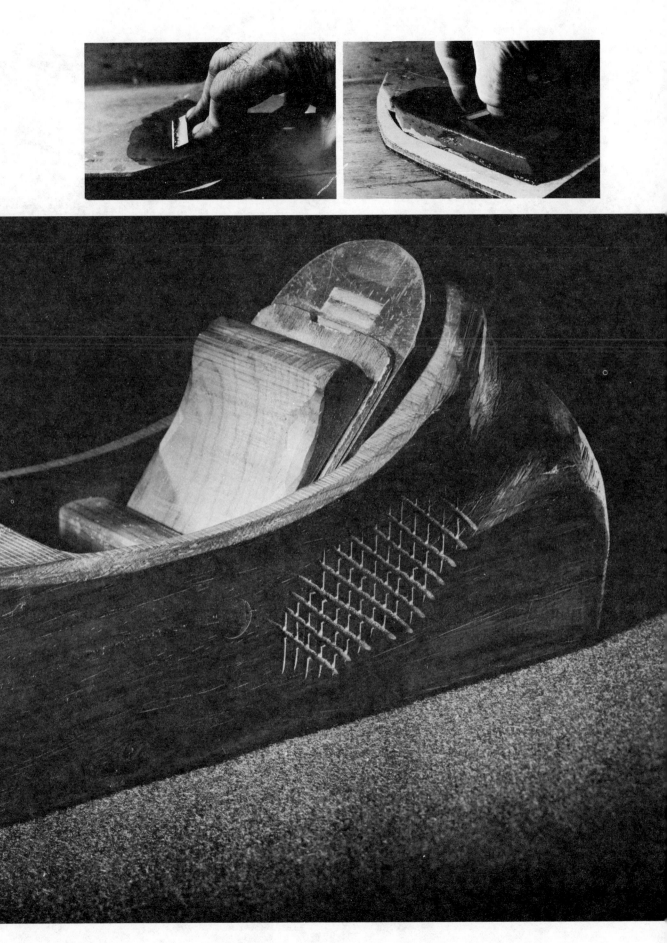

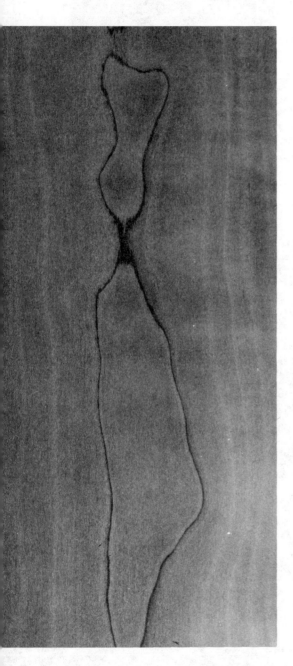

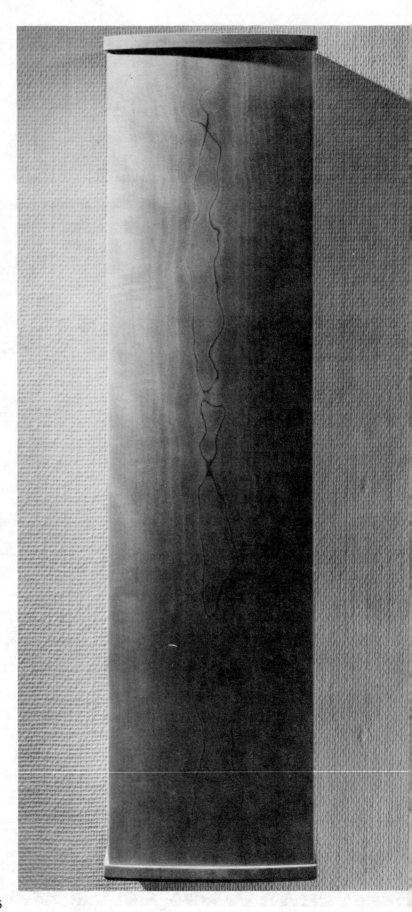

Wall cabinet in pearwood. Natural pearwood, mauve-colored, with the center pattern like pinkish smoke. I called it "Aladdin's lamp." The rippling grain was difficult to work with cutting tools, and had to be sanded—but very lightly. The detail shows the color patch on the door. Height 78 cm., width 20 cm., depth 13 cm. Untreated. 1970.

*Wall-hung bookcase of cherry wood, inside of drawer
in fragrant juniper. Length 54 cm., height 33 cm.,
depth 21 cm. Oil-polished. 1967.*

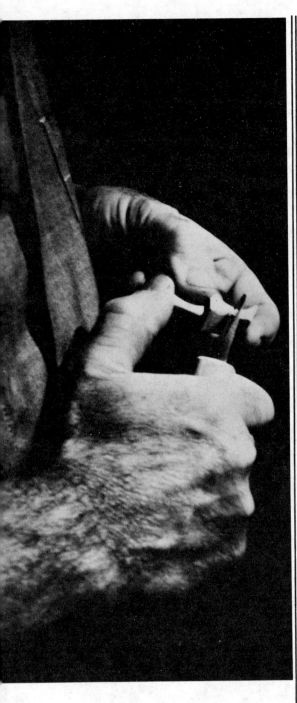

Above and opposite: *Carving a handle for a cabinet door. With the right small knife one can choose—and feel—the final shape.*

OF ALL THE TOOLS WE CABINETMAKERS HAVE

around us, the ones that are most neglected are knives. I don't know why this is so: perhaps because knives generally are rather crude and the work we associate with them is whittling. You know: the boy sitting on a stump, chewing a blade of grass as he whittles at a twig or a chip.

But knives, the way some of us experience them, are, alongside the chisel, plane, and spokeshave, really beautiful and versatile tools. Of course the first thing we have to do is to get away from the coarse knife we usually have around and try to get hold of—or better yet, make—some knives that we can do more detailed work with, knives that fit our hand and the ways of carving suited to making certain things.

Most knives have an awkward thick blade with a much-rounded tip: ours should be nicely tapered, thin and graceful. The whole knife with its definitely shaped handle is made to cut not away from, but *towards*. The carving we are talking about, small shapes and neat little roundings, minute details— this kind of carving is best done towards you. It is done with a very special action. You use your hand rather than your arm. You hold the knife close down and very tight. It should be a fairly short-bladed knife. Holding it firmly, you work it towards you with your fingers and forearm tense, gripping the knife exactly, firmly, and as you make these little cuts you are straining forward and yet at the same time there is a controlled braking because gripping tightly you can also stop at any time you want to twist your fingers and the blade and that way come out of any cut that seems to be going too deeply, or wrong.

Another thing you can do is turn the knife in your hand, away from you, and using the same tension cut away—not with the arm, but again with only the fingers. Holding the piece of wood in your left hand you can, with the left thumb, press against the top of the knife blade and "dip" that cut as you are making it away from you. These are smooth, strong movements your hands will be doing, and the thumb along the back of the knife gives force to the cut: you get a lot of power that way.

I'm talking about this because not having the right knife often keeps us from making simple discoveries and doing what we really want. Like using beautiful but very hard wood for small fine details: handles, consoles for shelves, little latches, and various other personal touches. But with a good knife these impulses become real and enjoyable. You are carving with a razor-sharp knife, keeping all your cuts under perfect control. This kind of work is among the most gratifying I know because there is somehow a *closeness*, the sense of being one with your strong fingers and your eye: your imagination, everything is there. It's a dance! All of you is working a little piece of bone-hard wood into some delicate shape that is a combination of usefulness and joy.

With small knives that have handles to fit your hand as you cut towards you, you can work very, very accurately, making clean cuts, shaping the piece so it does not have to be rough-sanded or filed, because working with sandpaper and files takes away from the pleasure of carving and also, I think, from some of the shapes themselves.

With time and interest comes skill: you learn to pivot the knife, twist it, use the very tip for the tiniest delicate shape. Your hands become hardened and awake, you can cut—crunch—deep and clean into a piece of secupira or hornbeam to round a friendly handle. The work comes easier, you are thinking less and feeling more, because you know your knife. And that is how it should be.

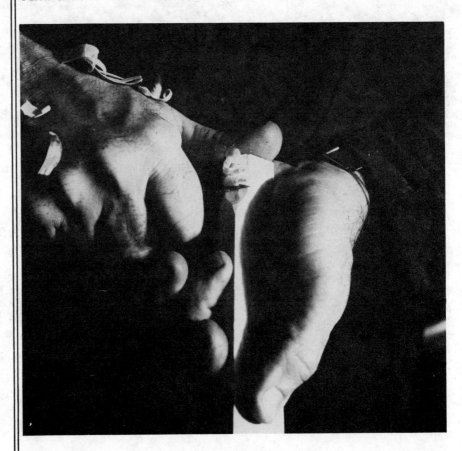

Small tools, made to fit the work one has done, and will do, with further pleasure.

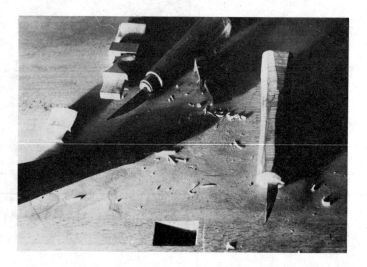

Details made with a knife.

Right: *The wooden door-catch at the top of a cabinet. Underneath is a small spring. Tension can be adjusted by the screw. This is the type of latch used on many of my cabinets.*

Below: *Door of a showcase cabinet. The protrusion on the door and the recess on the side of the cabinet make for easy opening without disturbing the simple lines of the door-front.*

41

AS A PERFECTIONIST, YOU EXIST ONLY SO LONG AS you are trying to make that perfect piece: on second thought, "perfect" is perhaps not quite what I mean, since the very word implies something beyond criticism and also remote from the warmth that keeps our work alive. But I have now and then wanted to do a piece—just one single thing—which would be the sum of all my efforts, and could justify my existence as a craftsman. Of course, that urge serves best while it is an illusion.

And what is that perfect piece? You complain because it eludes you—and are secretly glad because you have to complain. You mutter about a detail or a whole piece being not quite as you wanted, or hoped, to have it, and someone says: "It's fine as it is. Good to see, and to know that it was made by a human being."

Some mistakes you make, and correct. They often come when you have a bad day. And if you set things right, then the day ends better than it started—though it may end late.

But there is another kind of mistake: the one that lies between being a part of the human element at work—the "personal touch"—and something which you consciously did intend to be better, though not less human. It's a treacherous state to be in. You can stand in front of a piece all evening wondering, is it good? Yes, it is—but, what about *that* part: is it a mistake? What will happen if you back up and change it? You'll spend time (damn the time: that's not the point!), run the risk of spoiling the whole piece, and the result will be—a line: too straight to be quite alive? An edge: if you make it more even will this be a loss, or a noticeable gain? You are not so much worried about the effort or even risk involved, as over something else. This is where you've got to take a stand. Alone.

Working alone I do not have help, even when I need it. I do all the work myself. Partly this is because I don't like the idea of having someone do the dirty work for me, and then coming along, the artist guy, to do the finishing touches and put my John Henry on the piece. (This happens sometimes in a craft situation where young people think it is a privilege to go and study with a certain person—and they end up doing only the less interesting parts of the work.) The few people who spent time with me have been free: they have worked, exposed themselves to the environment, and done things they wanted to do. Though we would help each other and talk and spend a great deal of time together.

The other reason I don't have anyone working with me is vain and impractical, I know. But my feeling is that, for better or for worse, nobody else's hand, eye, or intuition will quite coincide with mine. Which does not mean mine are better: it's just that people are different.

I am not much for drawing; I can't say: "Here is a working drawing, make the piece according to this." My pieces are pieced together. All the little details, the way things add up, are unpredictable—or nearly so. It is a finger-tip adventure. Maybe someone else can do it better, I don't know. But this is me. When I put my initials on a piece (and I do so because people ask me to), that JK stands for me.

Sometimes I pleasantly forget. Then people remind me: I have had to go great distances because someone called me up and said, "We have a piece of yours and would like you to sign it." I owe it to them—I didn't use to think so, but now I realize that vanity aside, it is just a simple courtesy. So I inscribe my mark as small as I possibly can, some place underneath, where it is hard to find. Where it doesn't bother me—or anyone else.

My little mark, when I remember to put it there, is because I have done all the work.

WHAT IS IT LIKE WHEN YOU FIRST SET UP YOUR OWN
shop? Most of us begin with just a few very simple machines
that we have to make do with, and we go through the stage
of becoming a cabinetmaker; a stage that may last for years,
when we have to be inventive and make various simple tools.
During that time we have to try to think all the while, "This is
the kind of work that I'm going to stay with, and I don't want to
fight it. I don't want it to be something that is always a struggle.
I want the kind of work that I basically enjoy." There are aspects of it, of course—the dust and the dirt and the noise and
the sweat—that are dubious enjoyment, but still, in the midst
of it all, you want this thing that you feel is right and feels right.
You have got one or two simple machines. You've got your
hands, and your eyes, and your wood—this is what you are going to live with. If you are going to be a maker of musical
instruments—or whatever you are going to do—you will have
a tremendous use for fine knives, fine chisels, special little
tools that you might make, and small machines, to serve your
particular purpose. Of course, some of us are fortunate enough
to start with a shop that has what we need to save most of
our energy, and don't have to struggle quite as hard as other
people do. But for most it is a modest beginning and you accept
it and you want to enjoy it.

There is reason enough for a young person (or any person
really) setting up a shop, who wants to do what we call fine
craft in wood, to be doubtful about the final appreciation of his
audience. There isn't the establishment of mutual confidence.
The public does not always know, almost never knows, the
difference between the surface which can be produced in sensitive hands and with a sensitive eye, and the surface that
you have run off the jointer and belt-sanded. It is, I think in
some instances, as bad as that. Not always, of course; I don't
want to seem prejudiced in any way, but there is often a
tremendous lack of understanding. The more sensitive work
you do, the more afraid you will be in the first stages of your
life as a craftsman, because you will always be wondering, "Will
anyone ever come who will appreciate this? Here I am working, making these tools. Here I am listening to this old man tell-
ing about the difference between one surface and another,
one edge and another. Will it ever mean anything in my own
work and my own existence?" And I am perfectly aware that in
many instances it won't; not because you are insensitive,
but because of the climate, the craft climate, the attitude to-

wards wood. The fact that for years and years there hasn't been that much work done which is delicate and sensitive in this medium. There has been fine work done on a larger scale, heavier things a bit sculptured and large, yes. But small delicate things—an exquisite little jewelry box, a graceful little table, or a cabinet which is intended for lovely things and is itself a complement to them—this kind of work is rare, almost extinct. There is a true need to create a climate in which it can be done and appreciated.

Maybe this atmosphere of understanding will come; I can't say. But until it does come, work. Even when you are worried, work. Don't be pressured by originality. Don't lose time thinking that your work has to be wild and wooly, or slick. A nice four-legged table with pleasing and subtle, well-proportioned legs spaced right, the top in a pleasing form, is a beautiful thing, and rare. We don't necessarily have to make all kinds of sweeps and bends and such. Or worry if people say, "Well, it doesn't look . . . original," or, "I've seen a four-legged table almost like this before."

Around originality there is no doubt a law of diminishing returns; nowadays there has to be. Though maybe we are drowning not so much in the original as in the imitation, in just things. For many of us originality is a pressure; we are being pushed around by people wanting something new, different. Then there's the other pressure of doing the new without borrowing too much of the old, or at least without getting caught at it. Students are forever running to libraries to get various books—on peasant art, Scandinavian modern, Shaker, Colonial, Indian—one this and one that. They fill their heads with all these images, and then frantically try to come up with something of their own. As though you put these ingredients in a kettle, add water, stir, and cook for two hours. What do you get? Pottage. Pea soup.

It's a losing battle. And so exhausting. Stay out of it. It took me a long time to realize this, and accept my unoriginal self. Try to find the sort of people for whom there is another originality—that of the quiet object in unquiet times. It is rather ironic. We seem to have come the full turn, really. We're so up-tight that relaxation is something new, especially with regard to things. So a piece in low key, where the wood has its message and there is an idea and inspiration, where someone has worked honestly and well but with humility too—this is original. By contrast. That's the paradox I mean: let people take home a piece (cabinet or whatever) that is harmonious and well done, and simply live with it; they can have this little thing on a wall and come home and not have to open their eyes wide to exclaim, "Oh, great!" On the contrary, they come home with all these tensions, and this thing by its very being helps them relax somehow. They look at it; there is nothing wrong. They like it, it needs no explanation, no exclamation. They sit and relax and just live with it. All is well.

Perhaps because of my limited imagination, I have never felt that as a craftsman I could, or should, excite people in the usual sense of originality. If what I do achieves this other result, of soothing, or simply pleasing a certain kind of person, then perhaps everything is all right.

I try to remind my students of this, to give them confidence when I feel that they are worried about the future, under pressure, looking for new ideas rather than at the wood itself. Instead of touching the wood, turning it, looking at the other side, and then listening to it, these students are pressured by the belief that ideas have to come from outside and they have to be new and striking. So I try to restore their confidence and calm them and slow them down. I tell them that even if they won't make all that many things, or things that are all that striking, the things that they do will, if they are done right, appeal to the right person. And that is very, very important and should be encouraging. At least it should be reassuring, although sometimes one wonders; even as we reassure, we are at that very moment ourselves right in the middle of tension and contradiction because it is so difficult to establish any tangible evidence of the fact that this message is valid. Perhaps I and people like myself are doomed to fail in that respect because we are, in a way, contradicting a proven truth.

Very often students will come running to me, on Wednesday, let us say, with a sketch of something they have done. Their eyes are shining and they are raring to go and they have got to finish this whole thing and take it home to mother or the girlfriend or someone by Friday at the latest. And it is so difficult to explain to them that there will be this Friday, yes, but which Friday are we really talking about? There will be another Friday, and a Friday after that, and still another. And to get them to accept such an approach, to slow down, go into the work, let it come and see what happens is tremendously difficult, both for them and for me.

Yet I do believe that some are going to persevere and learn to think the other way: "I'm going to make these things because I want to make them, because I love the wood, because I have these fine tools, and I am just going to work and be happy doing it, no matter how long it takes, and learn all the time." I hope that, for these craftsmen, the beginning will come. People will notice and will see, even though they may not quite understand. They will say, "My goodness, this isn't what we always run into. This is somehow different." And maybe at first they will be puzzled. Maybe at first they won't even directly like the thing, but they will be aware of it. It just cannot be denied in its sensitive diversity. And out of that, maybe there will come a better time for our kind of craftsman.

Planing the side of an English brown oak cbinet. The oak had an unusual curl.

Jewelry box of Andaman padouk, fragrant as spices from the Indies. The sliding ring-holder was by request. Joints in this brittle, unyielding wood take extra time and patience. Hinges and other fittings of silver. Length 28 cm., width 21 cm., height 11 cm. Oil-polished outside, untreated inside. I found the padouk in 1962 and made the box in 1969—out of the last precious pieces.

49

Left and below: *Cabinet in ash with brownish heartwood at the deepest part of the concave door-curve. The irregular shape "changes" when one walks past the piece on the wall. The wood appeals to the hand. The pin-type brass hinges are specially made for me. Height 52 cm., width 56 cm., maximum depth 19 cm. Untreated. 1971.*

Opposite: *Showcase in doussie. There are glass shelves behind the three horizontal door-strips. Height 86 cm., width 22 cm., depth 14 cm. Oiled.*

ONE DAY AT SCHOOL WE WERE VIEWING SOME
slides of work by an applicant for a teacher's position. It was
good work. Professional, exact, up-to-date in tone. A bit so-
phisticated, perhaps, but well done. We were going through all
these slides when one of the students exclaimed: "Man, that's
a lot of work! How long has this guy been doing it?" I said
"About twelve years," and he said, "Wow! I thought it was
twice that long." Someone else laughed, "*You* it would take
forever, Ace."

It *was* a lot of work we were looking at. Time and effort, day
in and day out: that's what this kind of cabinetmaking is about.
Not just a great piece once in a while, and then a long row of
ordinary stuff dragging you down, but fine things all along. For
a few craftsmen this makes sense; for most it is a frustration.
You've either got the patience, or you haven't. Some of us
have the self-discipline it takes, others don't. One chap wants
results, period. Another is willing to sweat and wait as long
as necessary to do what has to be done. Ours is one of the most
time-consuming crafts of all, but for him it's no problem:
things have to be done, and you have to do them if you are ever
going to see the rewards. Now. And again, and again: the same
things—more or less, depending on how personal your touch
is, how much skill you have. Because skill in this craft means
being able to do interesting variations on almost any theme.
That helps.

Good cabinetmaking is usually a complex task. It is a lot of
concentrated thinking and exact moving. Think wrong,
and you've probably ruined something, maybe a week or a
month's work. Move wrong, and you can lose a finger or hand.
Especially if you get impatient.

There's a lot involved—not just money, either—and you've
got to be realistic about it all, and make the big choice before
it is too late. You can do woodworking for a living, as just
another job, probably in a production setup someplace. Then
there are reproduction carving, and woodturning: these are
valid and almost painless ways to make a living. Or you may be
an oddball who wants to do your own thing, your way. Then
you are looking for trouble! Consider: who appreciates quality
nowadays? The bills are piling up, time is going by. You must
choose. If this means going on doing your best then, no matter
what else—talent or mere energy or whatever—you are in
for a lot of just plain work. (Well, hopefully not too plain). It's
something you can't get around and should not even hope to

get around—unless you either use other people, or do bad work, or both. Often if you do one, you end up doing both.

The good thing is to develop your habits and discipline and get a flow in the work so that it all makes long-term sense. There is no way of making it easy, though you can make some of it easier and most of it enjoyable by being friends with what you are doing. You learn more that way, and the work shows it. Which in turn helps to keep you going, without thinking about all the time and effort it takes: a large part of the battle is getting to the point where you no longer worry about the time and work involved. Still, for some of us it is too much. In the long run we can't do it. This is understandable. And this is why, when we see a fine piece of cabinetmaking, we should look closely, and think about what it means, and remember that it is not just pieces of wood put neatly together, but a measurable part of an honest craftsman's life.

Sawing rough stock for consoles to support shelves. The final shape of each is carved by hand and fitted to the hole-size in the cabinet.

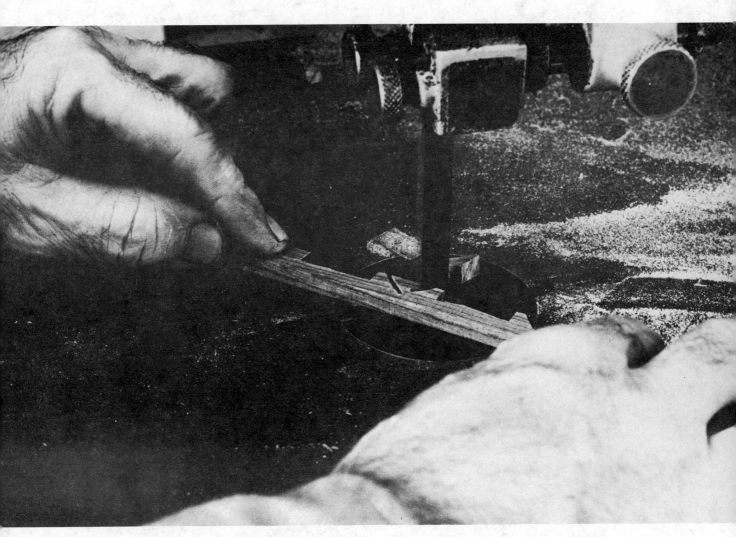

53

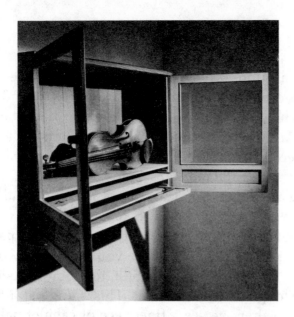

Wall cabinet of Oregon pine for a classic Italian violin, used daily by a member of the Stockholm Philharmonic orchestra. Sliding trays are for bows, rosin, etc. The detail of the sliding trays shows the finger-grips at the ends of the trays. Height 55 cm., width 88 cm., depth 23 cm. Oil-finished. 1969.

Chess table of solid wood, intended to have a quality feel and sound. Playing surface of natural pearwood and Rio rosewood, body of secupira, drawer of maple. A difficult, disciplined piece to make, but rewardng since it has proved its purpose well, and "feels right" to use. The details show the top, the legs and cross-piece, one of two drawers for chessmen, and the through-tendons at the top of the legs, which are diagonally wedged towards the middle of the table. Length 78 cm., width 65 cm., height 72 cm. Untreated. 1970.

A FAIR PART OF MY LIFE AS A CRAFTSMAN HAS BEE
shadowed with doubts. Doubts as to whether I was meant to·
this kind of thing. Still more doubts as to whether I could do
well enough. After all, I was brought up on excellence: wha
ever you do, do it well. As I got far enough into the work
have certain hopes, the doubts by contrast became even
stronger. Finally there was the worst doubt of all, when a
times I would ask myself, "Whom are you fooling? What if you
work is fair but not really good, not so good that any fineI
tuned person will simply have to respond?"

Granted, most of us go through this, trying to find ourselv
and at the same time survive. Some people, artists of a kin
can go on and on and on and say to themselves and to othe·
"What I am doing may not be acknowledged during my
time, but after I am gone it *will* be acknowledged. It *is* art.'
These people are able to turn their wives into the streets ar
let the children go barefoot and get bad teeth, and still they w·
persevere in their work. But for me, it's always ended in tl
question, "Persevere to what end? At whose expense?" Th
kind of thinking would fill me with all sorts of fears and
doubts.

I was brought up on responsibility and self-discipline, pro
ably to excess. So I would stand and look at my work, and
I'd weigh it. Go into myself, ask questions. But these were on
my eyes, my intuition, and my opinion. Very often they
weren't enough. Alone in the house, I would panic, stare at n
workbench, then go upstairs, make a cup of coffee, sit sip-
ping it looking out at the birch trees, winter-bare and trem
bling. In the midst of fear an undercurrent would begin,
the feeling that is so difficult to define. Down in my worksho
again, the sum total of values once given to me said, "This
isn't bad." As I worked and got on, maybe there was some o·
who said the same, "This is not bad." The pieces I made weren·
all that many, but they won friends. And not just my friend·
The encouragement of my friends was helpful, but the piece
won their own friends. These were, by coincidence or some
thing else, people with whatever it is that allows one to follo·
one's feelings consistently. Call it class or taste or intuition
you find it being discussed in articles on art and culture,
etc., etc., but discussed by others. Anyway, people whom I re
spected and felt I could rely on appreciated my work. So
each piece and the people involved kept me going. It's alway
been personal, not just between me and what I'm doing, bu

with me and all those who have been involved, who have looked me up, left me little messages of encouragement, bought the few first pieces that I made. It's all quite simple. Except that there were times of silence when the telephone didn't ring and no one came and there wasn't any mail; when I thought, felt, *knew* that others were making it easy for themselves and getting away with it, using reputations and names and trends to advantage. Oh, it is easy to be sorry for oneself on a "high" level!

So I would sweep the clean floor once, twice, three times; sharpen tools that were already perfectly sharp; look at a plank and another, maybe saw some piece only to imagine I was starting to spoil it, and get all my impressions of wood and work and idea mixed up into a frenzy. Then something else would step in, compelling. And I'd suddenly rush out into the fresh air, and I'd walk and walk. There were woods and a lake not too far away. It was an hour's walk to peace and quiet. Along the path through the woods, things would settle a bit. I'd begin to think about one of the planks, and realize that perhaps I could save it. Maybe I was wrong in my dark impression of those first cuts that I'd made. Already I was beginning to link a clear idea to that particular piece of wood, to what the cut had revealed and the work that might come from the combination of that wood and this idea. Or maybe it was just the fact that under the self-pity and the fear I knew, and I know now, that I am a very lucky person. When I feel lucky in the total sense, I also feel very much ashamed for my weaknesses and the times when I have doubted, the instances when I've wasted a bit of what is most valuable in life. Time has passed, and I'm somewhere on a hill now. Anywhere I look around is down. Along the rest of the way, I must be less afraid. And more grateful.

Once I used to get wood from far places, and take for granted that two, three, or four years would pass before it would be ready to use. Now, four years is a long time. I'm still excited at the thought of writing to a friend in São Paulo and asking for some secupira or goncalo alves. But now my excitement is shaded by apprehension, almost regret. A half a year to get here, three years to dry . . . and time is passing. I am sad, not at the thought of getting old, but because I might miss so much lovely wood. Four years. Statistics predict I will still be around:

59

instinct wags a warning finger. How strong will my back b[e]
then, how steady my hands and eye?

I don't want to overemphasize these fears, but they are
there. This has its good side, too, because you start conservin[g]
your energy and maybe are more efficient at your work.
You've got the feeling, "Let's not think ten years ahead, let'[s]
concentrate on the present!" Still, nature sends you signals,
and some are a bit sober.

I don't love working—it is working well that I love. Henc[e]
the soberness: I don't want to go on being a cabinetmaker afte[r]
I start to make excuses, to say, 'We-ell, you know, it isn't bad[,]
but if you had come to me three or four years ago I'd have don[e]
a better job. But of course, I am sixty-two, and considering,
it's not bad. Almost as good as I used to do. . . ."

I won't allow myself that: I'll quit when it's not going just a[s]
I know it should.

Right: *Maple. A sawn log may contain six heavy
planks of which two can be used.*
Opposite: *Detail of a maple showcase cabinet showing lock and key at side.*

Music-stand "for two." Natural pearwood. Double rack folds flat (see detail). There are two drawers, "one" handle. The drawers are in partiture size, and can slide out both sides of the stand. Each half has a through-tendon wedged on the inside of the drawer. Length 68 cm., width 41 cm., height (opened) about 105 cm. Untreated. 1970.

63

Music stand in lemonwood. This one has a vertical-pattern rack. Bevels on the legs change to enhance the flaring, tapered shape. Same size as the pearwood music stand. Oiled. 1970.

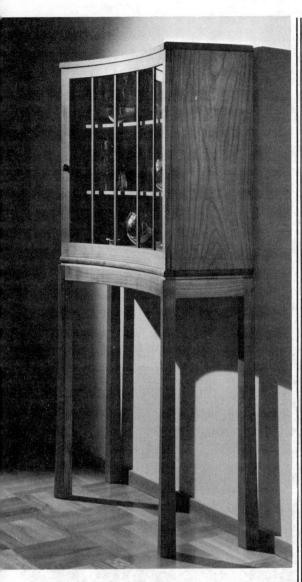

Showcase cabinet in cherry wood. Wide door with upper and lower curves laminated. This cabinet is a larger descendant of the cabinet on page 121. Height 153 cm., width 92 cm., maximum depth 26 cm. The honey-colored wood is oiled outside, polished inside. 1974.

OUR MACHINES ARE TREACHEROUS. AND I DON'T

just mean they bite; they do. But the real treachery is more elusive. On the one hand they help the cabinetmaker greatly; on the other, they corrupt him. Somewhere between these two ways there is a sensible and sensitive balance which our craftsman must try to find before it is too late.

My machines are not many and not large, but they are adequate in relation to the work we do together. I rely on them and pamper them: they in turn cut clean and straight. By now we know exactly where we stand, they and I.

A visitor the other day expressed surprise over these machines—they collided with his impression of the romantic craftsman. He was from England, and I think he brought a bit of a William Morris attitude with him. Here now was this man about whom he had heard, and no doubt the fellow did everything by hand and had a very picturesque and primitive workshop. As he came in and saw my modest but fine equipment he exclaimed, "Oh, so you do have machines!" And I said "Why, of course. How else?" And indeed, what would be the purpose of ripping up the rough stock by hand, doing a vast amount of preparatory work with much effort and little accuracy, and then charging someone for a day or two or three of extra labor. That would be ridiculous, not only from the point of view of cost, but also because of the nature of the work involved. The task of getting the wood to the stage where you can begin to foresee a result and the so-called creative work with fine hand tools is exhausting. If you use up all your energy needlessly doing the hard labor by hand, then usually you won't have the strength and the clarity of purpose to do that fine part later on—when it really counts.

This was not evident to me when I started. Or maybe, simply not having the means to buy them, I minimized the importance of certain machines. Anyway, I did buy a good little bandsaw. For a while I was alone with this saw, a few odd planes, and the first pieces of wood I had gathered. I had to hand-plane everything right from each rough plank. I'd take a running start and then throw myself along that plank on the workbench, trying to get one side and one edge squared up so I could start bandsawing the rest. Oh yes, I did learn something doing it. But I almost killed myself in the bargain. With a jointer I would have been spared half the torture.

On the other hand, in schools where you begin learning at a time when most of us are very vulnerable, there is an overabundance of woodworking machinery. All these temptations! You watch your friends using them. You have an idea about the shape and nature of a certain detail, maybe you even sense that there should be a way for your hands to interpret it. A sound instinct makes you doubt any other way. But there is no clear sight of the tool you need, only the vague notion that it should be there. While here are all these machines which everyone is using, even for such small details. So you leave your impulse and go along with reason. And that shape, those curves, edges—what might have been your expression—becomes the product not so much of enthusiasm and adventure as of efficiency.

Somewhere at the outset we need to have our unreasonable dream warmly justified, our enthusiasm kept alive by strong fingers guiding a sharp tool. Yet if you reject the machine, still another danger arises. Working by hand only will not necessarily express what you want to say and it can knock you out by the sheer weight of the work. What good is the sensitiveness of your fingertips if you have started wrong? If the joints you intended to be clean and crisp are a disappointment? If "Made by hand" doesn't quite say what you wanted to say? What compensation is a carved shape or a neat detail for an earlier failure?

Each of us alone must determine the balance. Say to the machine, "You and I have come this far together. . . . Thank you, machine—and goodbye. I am going to do the rest without you. Because I have those beautiful tools. Because with them in my hands I know better what I want to say, and how to say it my way—not yours."

At some fateful point it all hangs by a thread. Or perhaps on the way a shaving comes off a fine tool.

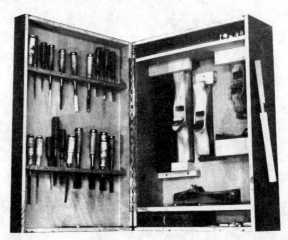

A few of the hand-tools I keep, hoard—and pamper.

Writing-reading table in maple. The top is adjustable, from flat to desired angle. The lip along the edge of the top "curls over" so that even one thin sheet of paper will remain in place. The single drawer runs lengthwise. Height (with top flat) 72 cm., width 54 cm., length 80 cm. Oil finish. 1971.

Raya.

GROWING UP WITH ANIMALS IS ENRICHING, BUT

also habit-forming: later on in life, if you aren't with them, you miss them. In Alaska when I was a boy, it was dogs, dogs all the time. Half-wild malamutes barking and snarling at each other, howling at the moon and the Northern Lights. One of mine pulled me breathtakingly along twisting trails. Now and then he'd stop, and peer back at me and cock his head. He had two round white spots above his eyes. I've forgotten his name.

After that it was travel, and some years without pets. But now with a house and a workshop I can have pets—this time, cats. Two black ones. Kirri is old and wise and aloof; Raya is young, stupid, and friendly. She lies on my workbench with one eye closed and refuses to move. I can be working, cutting joints, bang, bang, an inch from her wet little nose, and she won't budge. Sometimes she sits on my shoulder, or if I'm leaning over she will drape herself like a boa and purr contentedly. She doesn't want to get off: I have to lean way over and slide her onto the bench, where she moves near the warm lamplight and lies down again. For a while.

I'll be working at my bench and suddenly there will be a prrrr sound as Raya comes in to the basement through the little hatch in the door. There's an opening there with a piece of cloth over it to keep out the draft and she pushes this aside and comes in and says, "Prrrrr," and looks at me and wants to go upstairs. So I go upstairs and there is usually some nice tidbit for her, a piece of fish, for example. But very often she fools me: she just wants me to go upstairs and sit with her or talk to her, I suppose because she isn't hungry. Then I will ask her, "Whom have you eaten?" Because she does come through that hatch sometimes with a very special sound and bringing her catch, and then she will come to the middle of the workshop floor with a paw on a gray bit of fluttering life and she will look up at me with narrow eyes, waiting for approval. What is one to do?

Twice I have saved a bird and, together with Raya, seen it find the window that I have thrown open, and disappear. I'd apologize to Raya and she'd sniff about on the floor and maybe there would be a few feathers still left and she would mutter her frustrations, but Raya is Raya and she soon forgets. And then she jumps up on the bench and sits there blinking at me. She likes to have me bend over a little bit and then she will nudge my beard with her muzzle, rub me, and then start to purr. And if I stroke her she will flop over on the bench with a beautiful twisting motion, just like an otter playful in the water, and she will purr again and want me to scratch her tummy, which of course I do. Another time she will just sit on the floor and look at me, and strange thoughts come. You realize how vulnerable a little animal is. How totally dependent upon goodness and patience and a bit of fun together. It's a little bit frightening and at the same time very gratifying.

By pure chance she is living her happy life with us and did not, when she was a kitten, go to someone else. That, too, can start a chain of thought and I will look at her and she will look at me for a while and then she will just walk off and go upstairs and find the most comfortable chair in the living room and there I'll find her a bit later, curled in a little black ball.

Raya.

A STORY THAT HAS STUCK IN MY MIND AND AF-
fected me is one of the innumerable anecdotes about a legend-
ary cabinetmaker in Denmark called Peder Moos. He is gone
now but this story has helped me and it just might help someone else. It's about a woman in Stockholm who, at the time that
Peder Moos was fairly well known, wrote him a letter and
asked him whether he would make her a cabinet. Several
months went by and she did not get a reply, so finally she called
him on the telephone and repeated her request. He muttered
something about well, yes, he would do that, or at least he
would think about it. Several months went by and still no
answer so the lady wrote him a card reminding him of her
request, and again she did not get a reply.

Then one day, the story has it about a year and a half after
she had originally contacted him, there came a postcard from
Peder Moos, "I have made a piece for you." The lady, of course,
was tremendously excited; she took the first possible train
down to Copenhagen and then to the smallish town where
Peder Moos lived and worked. She went to his shop, met him—
and there was a chair. The lady looked at the chair, and took it
and paid for it, and went home very, very happy.

I am nourished by that tale, and it has helped me in the sense
that it has encouraged a bit of free play in what I do. My own
way is not that of Peder Moos; it is more hesitant. It is simply that if I am making something for someone, I ask them to
leave me free to interpret the idea and the request. At the same
time, I like to leave *them* free, I do not ask for an assurance
that they will buy the piece when I have finished it; I ask for no
downpayments or a promise of any kind in writing. No one
has yet deceived me—maybe because it's not worth deceiving
someone so simple-minded. Anyway, either I and these people
feel we have contact and this thing between us is interesting
and congenial and may result in a piece that we will both
appreciate and enjoy, or else there is not this contact and then
there simply is no use continuing. It has worked out well,
partly because of my very cautious way of working, the methods that I have evolved, the step-by-step technique where I
can back up and look at my work and correct it and then carefully go ahead again. And if I am doing something for any
specific person or persons, then I usually ask them to visit me
several times during the process of work and look at the thing
and judge it with me. They enjoy the experience; afterwards
they look back on these visits and remember participating

in the process.

But, of course, people who come and request something are a luxury. I have not survived by waiting for commissions, for visitors, or for the telephone to ring. For years I have worked just on the basis of an idea that I might have, some object that would be usable. If I had waited for commissions and all sorts of interesting things to happen, I would not have survived the first year or two when I had a tiny shop and nothing happened. I worked from one piece to the next, buying a plank or two when I could, selling my work for a pittance, and going through the process of humiliation at times and perhaps exaggerated gratitude at others when someone would offer me almost a fair price for something that I had done. It was a very strange time; I was fluctuating between hope and despair, but always working.

Looking back on it, I realize that not everyone would have done it so consistently. I survived by simply refusing to do things because people wanted me to do them, or resorting to some sort of small series production and doing things multiply—two or three or four at a time. I made one object at a time because of the wood, because of the tools, with a certain idea and hope, and somehow these objects won friends and gradually, gradually, my confidence and experience increased. But for a very long time, it was touch and go. Even now, although people may think that I've got it made and things are going fine, even now I am only carrying my end of the plank. Someone else who is sharing life with me and has believed from the beginning in what I am trying to do is carrying the other end of that plank.

I suppose that one of the most common presumptions about anyone who works individually as a craftsman, especially one who makes functional ojects, is that he is competing with some other sources of production—industry or small industry or the semi-industrialized craftsman, the one who makes several of a kind and has in some way standardized production. I have never looked at it that way. The element of competition has never even worried me, because from the start, I suppose, I realized wood contains so much inspiration and beauty and rhythm that if used properly it would result in an individual, a unique object. I got into this intimate relationship with wood and tools and was very happy, and this confirmed to me that the work of my fingertips and my eyes (most wonderful tools) should be visible and tangible in every way to

Dovetails with intentional "tension" in the spacing: closer towards the outer edges of the piece (a cabinet-carcase), a bit farther apart in the middle.

the hand, the eye, to all the senses. The fact that I somehow realized this before it was too late gave me ground to stand upon, the beginning of a sense of identity.

I didn't worry about competing, especially after I read David Pye's book, *The Nature and Art of Workmanship;* he confirmed for me that the true craftsman is not at all in competition with any other source of production. His sole reason for being—his raison d'être—is that he offers people something that industry and other more rational means of production cannot give them. Granted, David Pye has a very definite concept of what craftsmanship is. He doesn't talk in terms of artiness or art or convenience. As he uses the word craftsmanship, it contains a great deal. Which is reassuring. What I have tried to do is merely be consistent, in other words, realize that if I'm going to do something, it should be personal, and contain all of myself. Then all of it has to be done in a consistent, uncompromising way. Somehow, instead of that being an added strain to me, it became a source of relief. I realized this was the way it should be, and the problem somehow disappeared. I think it was the beginning of harmony in my work and in my living with my work: I realized that this was the only way that I could and should do it.

What I have tried to do in all my objects is to not allow myself to think, "Well, here's the back side of the drawer and, you know, a drawer is not meant to be pulled all the way out; so if it is not quite as presentable as the front, it might not matter all that much." Or, "This is the back of the cabinet and if it is veneered or if it is not quite as well polished as the inside, it is really not all that significant because it will, after all, be against the wall."

I think there is another way of looking at work, namely, that people who buy objects made by persons like myself don't just want a table because they need a table or a cabinet because they need to keep certain things in it. They can get mass-produced or semi-mass-produced products that will solve those furnishing problems. They are looking for something more. I don't like to think that they are looking for art: certainly I am not thinking of art when I am working and I don't enjoy the aura, the atmosphere, of arty people and arty conversation. What the people who are attracted to my work enjoy is that when they are at home in the evening, and perhaps have friends visiting, they can approach one of these objects and make small discoveries: they can pull a drawer all the way out

74

The back of a drawer. The solid wood bottom is shaped and grooved into sides and front piece. Doussie.

and turn it around and look at the back of it, and it is consistent and neat and honestly done, and they will note that the bottom is solid wood, and it is fitted in a particular way and it has a nice little profile running along the edges, and that the back of the cabinet is a frame and panel and solid wood, never veneer, and they will be able to experience a handle or a console that supports the shelves or run their fingers along the front edge of a shelf or even the underside of a shelf and find a meaning there. Whatever detail strikes them or appeals to them will be consistent. They, and their friends too, will perhaps be amused by all of this and they will say, "Look, you see this—see this little thing—now look at this other detail; I didn't notice this before myself, although I have had this piece for quite a while. . . . Look at the underside of this table: the fellow who made this really cared."

I think this consistency—the fact that these little objects perhaps have what Professor Pye called diversity, things to be discovered as you get closer to them—is of crucial importance. There should be more to it than an architectural experience, and I am encouraged by the fact that I am somehow making a game of this, putting in these little details which are not just superfluous and there for effect, but are a part of the whole experience. A handle becomes an adventure and a challenge; so too a little latch on a door and the joints in a drawer. All these things can be many-sided and interesting and I do them differently from time to time; each is somehow always new to me. I don't have patterns. Nor predetermined measurements and standards of any kind. I am always starting from scratch and the things that I discover making the piece, the diversity that I experience working, is left in the piece, and others then can make their own little amusing discoveries and live with the pieces on a very friendly and warm and intimate basis. I think that the way I regard wood assures the fact that the piece will age gracefully and that usage will give it a patina. Like a person, it will have its moods. And certainly if one cares about people, then moods are a part of experiencing them.

•

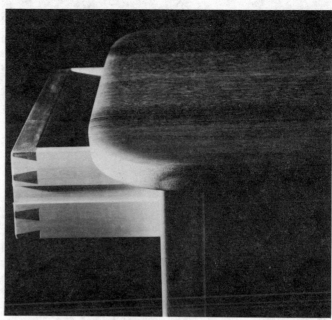

...nall chair-side table of Italian walnut. ...he softness of the top and legs is a part ... the total shape—friendly, since one ... apt to bump into such a table, there be-...des one's chair. The details show the ...rough-drawer, with sides and bottom ... solid maple. Height 59 cm. width ...2 cm, length 57 cm. Waxed. 1973.

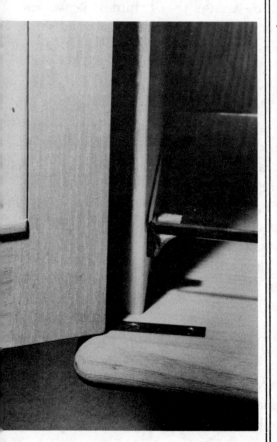

Wall cabinet of Swedish yellow ash. The grain works with the shape and proportions. The detail shows the carved wood consoles which support the shelves. Height 67 cm., width 44 cm., maximum depth 17 cm. The wood with its delicate texture is untreated. 1969.

FOLLOWING ARE SOME COMMENTS ABOUT PIECES of mine which were shown at various places during the years 1971–74.

Probably the objects themselves should speak; I hope that in a sense they do. However, I believe there is an unnecessary distance between the public and what the best crafts have to offer. Often in our haste we neglect to look at things in a way that tells us what they really are, and lets us sense how they came to be. We craftsmen seldom make things without premeditation, as a part of life around us; that life in its complexity excludes such naturalness. It is a long way back to the village blacksmith and potter, who did their work completely naturally. In those days the reasons were obvious; people looked directly, and saw, even before they comprehended. Still, there *is* a meaning in what we do today, and a reason why we do it in a particular way. My comments should not be taken as an urge to mediate, or to explain—much less to analyze—but only as a wish to help bridge the gap which our times have created between us and such objects; to help you see better and perhaps imagine that you can touch.

There is the small showcase cabinet in Swedish ash with the door set slightly at an angle. I use Swedish ash because ordinary ash as a wood is rather uninteresting. The common variety of ash, which is mostly white wood, rather coarse grained and with very little pattern, is not exciting at all.

But this Swedish yellow ash, as we call it, contains quite a bit of life and color and structure. Structure, when you play with it, use it, can become rhythm. What I mean when I say rhythm is the play of the lines and shadings in the wood. And I hope that this is something people will be aware of in my things. At some times it may be more apparent than at others, but it is a conscious attempt to use in the piece I am making the colors and texture and tensions of the material itself.

The whole point of departure is different from what is perhaps common in the sense that it is a guessing, a seeking, instead of just following an intention professionally. I do not say to myself, "Well, I've drawn something to be done in wood. Now let's get this or that color wood and do it! I know from the drawings that it is going to be a fine and exciting thing." Most of my work comes not from drawings but from an idea

Detail of Swedish yellow ash wall cabinet: mid-point with door-frames and bottom piece. This seems simple . . . .

I have. Something that is both a guess and a hope. There may be a rough sketch, yes, but I am not bound from the beginning. I am groping toward something, composing as I go along. I have an idea, more often than not a function, and always the wood is there to guide me.

Now this showcase, I hope, will do justice to some collected small objects that most people have and that perhaps have been just lying around the house. They will be gathered in this little case which in a sense will be *their* house. So that all through the process of choosing the wood, sawing it, arranging it, rearranging it, I am making a guess and then taking the next step and then guessing again and hoping that I will be right.

This cabinet has a balance, I hope; a sort of harmony. I don't want perfect symmetry. I have a built-in resistance to the all-too-symmetrical and stiff. But within a form or proportion it is good to feel harmony, a balance that you can say is harmonious, not discord. Not something you will feel is wrong, but a thing to put you at ease.

To be at ease is a kind of thrill, I guess. A pleasantly different feeling during these hectic times. We are all so rushed and impressed by startling things that I think it is truly a deep satisfaction to experience, now and again, something that just puts you at ease, that gives you a moment of peace and contemplation.

The sides of this little cabinet, as you see, have a bit of the lighter part of the wood, the sapwood, in the back. It could be the other way. Perhaps the sapwood could be in the front but then the door would have to be much lighter than it is now, too, and I don't think this would be quite as good. As it is, the door has a more definite form, clearer lines with the darker grain working intentionally into the shape of the door. Besides, the cabinet sort of leaves the wall with this light back edge. It floats!

I am constantly working with these elements: light and dark shading. A tension in the wood and then another tension to respond to it, to play with it in a way that I feel has some meaning.

The whole cabinet is done in solid wood. The back piece as you see, is solid, paneled. The pattern of the back piece is very decisive for this cabinet. I made one other such cabinet, and the back piece was a rather straight-lined pattern. But the grain of this one is like the trunks of two trees, curving,

Details of Swedish yellow ash cabinet. Inside of cabinet door. Strips holding glass are butted, not mitred, at the corners. Handles, carved from secupira, encourage one to use finger-tips when opening the small doors.

first inward from the root, and then a bit out toward the first branches. And this gives the cabinet a very definite character. The ash is at its best natural and untreated.

If someone were to come to me now and say, "Make me a cabinet like this and I will pay you whatever you wish," I would simply not be able to do it. I would have to say, "Well, perhaps someday, if and when I find a plank out of which I can get a pattern like this which I know is best for this cabinet. Then perhaps I'll do it. But until then, whatever the offer, I must say 'No!'"

Details, even the smallest ones, are an integral part of my work. Within the little details there is a search for meaning, too, that I hope enriches the finished piece. The rear pegs that hold the shelves, the ones that are in the back of the cabinet, are fitted into the sides at a slight angle forward, so that if you should want to move them up or down, the back of the cabinet will not be in your way.

And the strips that hold the glass in the doors are *not* mitered in the corners like a picture frame: the top and bottom pieces are slightly thicker and wider and there is a nicely overlapping joint, which I think is more harmonious. It feels better to me.

Speaking about feeling: there are the door handles. The handles are intended to be felt by the fingertips. I shouldn't like people to approach the cabinet callously or aggressively. The handle expresses an intent, a wish that someone should take it very gently, just between the thumb and forefinger, and open the door. Because the whole cabinet is light and airy, and there is no reason to be rough about it.

The idea of the door set slightly at an angle is logical: there is no bad reflection of light. In other words, there's always one side of the door, at least, that does not reflect the light, and I think this is desirable. You don't get the disturbing glare of one continuous flat surface of glass.

There is a chain of thought behind everything, but it's not drawn and calculated in the manner that a professional designer or architect would do it. It is an idea and a guessing, step by step. Sometimes I have more luck, sometimes less.

Another little showcase cabinet with glass is in bird's eye maple. Bird's eye maple is a rarity in Sweden. It doesn't grow there as far as I know. This, no doubt, is an import item. It comes from the Continent somewhere. I found it in a pile of diverse maple which a company in Stockholm had imported. There is more of it in the United States, as I discovered when I taught at the School for American Craftsmen.

This is the second such cabinet I have made. The first was for a lady who had some items of silver done by a woman silversmith—very feminine items, really. One was a necklace, and she wanted to hang it in a cabinet. I made that one in pear wood: pear wood is, as I see it, a little bit feminine in character.

The sides of the cabinet are not flat. They are slightly curved, and there is a softness about them. The curve came that way, almost of itself. It is hand-planed. Both pear and maple are fine to plane, as you can tell by touching the planed surfaces, which I hope you will want to do.

There is quite a bit of wood when you see the piece from in front. It has more the sense of soft weight than the other showcase cabinet, which is mostly light lines. The shelves here are of wood. I tried glass and it didn't work. It was not harmonious. Whereas if you put wooden shelves in the ash cabinet, it would be a failure. It would chop up the cabinet—cut it into shaded, unpleasant sections. So the shelves are a guess at first.

I have been very lucky with the wood here. It's a rarity, and I think that its shimmer and its bird's eye pattern and the thin streaks of color in the back piece all blend well with the idea of the cabinet itself.

Here, too, the door handle is such that it encourages use with care. As you open and close the door you will notice the little wooden peg down at the bottom, which keeps the door from sagging. And then, above, the little spring catch made of wood with a metal spring under it, which keeps the tension on the door. So you get the feeling of wood against wood as the door closes, which is a soft "swish" and not a metallic "clang."

People like this cabinet very much. It is waxed with a very special English wax, a synthetic product. And waxed, this bird's eye maple is, I think, at its best. The surfaces can be freshened up with just a bit of very fine steel wool if there should be any blemishes or smudges on it.

Opposite: Small showcase in bird's eye maple. Sides are softly convex, upper shelf curves inward, both shelves have front edge beveled. Door with handle opens comfortably from left to right. Height 56 cm., width 38 cm., depth 14 cm. Waxed.

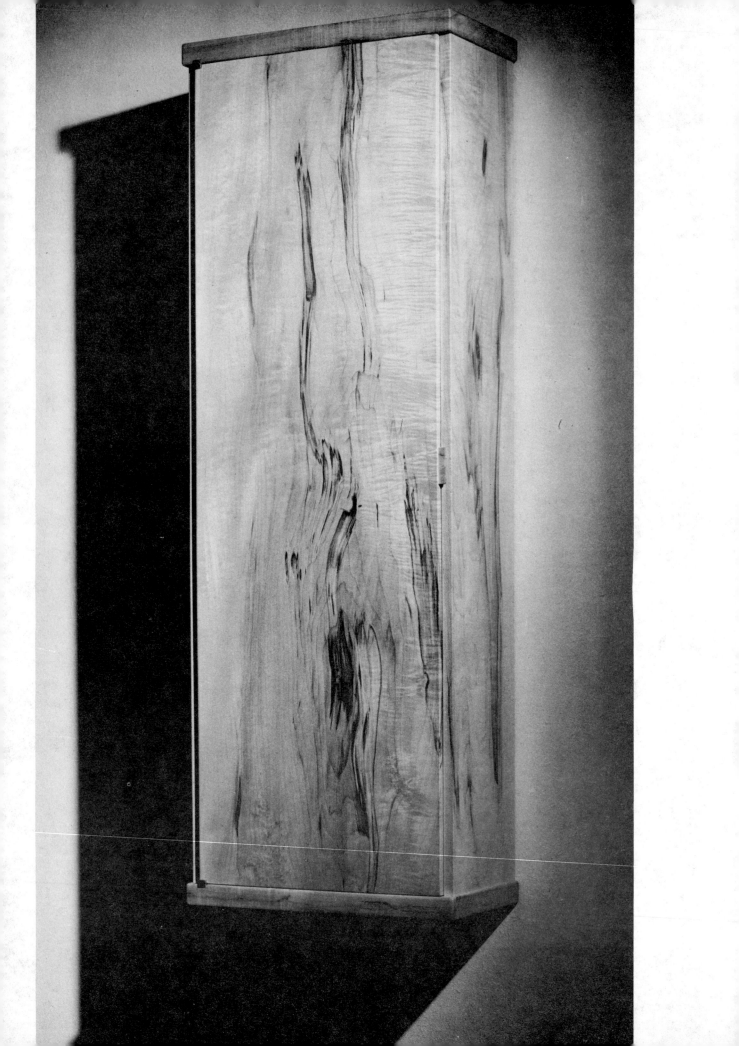

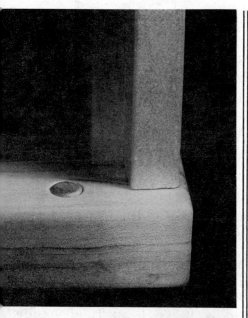

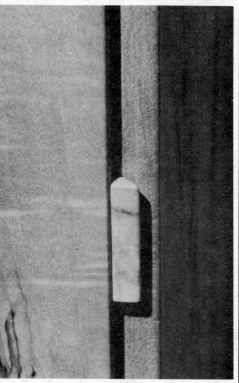

Third, there is the cabinet in Swedish maple with a very unusual greenish-whitish-mauve swirl. I call this cabinet "the precious stone," because this is an example of rarity in wood. My part in it has been that I have saved the wood. Or rather, a bit of it.

What you see in this cabinet is what is left of four planks from a whole trunk of a tree that was sawn for me and which was mostly cracks and checks, and couldn't be used.

I had this flitch-cut log in my workshop for about two years and kept looking at it, and picking and poking, and when finally I got to sawing, it was one heartbreak after another. The most beautiful parts of the planks were full of tiny checks. Not honest cracks, but treacherous little checks, hardly visible. I had to give most of the wood away.

So this little cabinet is kind of a precious stone in wood, you might say, and I don't know how you would evaluate it. If you have a diamond or an emerald that is extremely beautiful, it is worth a great deal, and the person who has faceted it and polished it isn't really important. It is the stone that contains the value.

And this is as close to wood as a valuable or curiosity as I should like to come. My contribution here is not great, but it involved some patience. I found the wood; I saved what could be saved, and here it is.

"Precious stone" cabinet of Swedish maple, all that is left of a small log, mostly cracked beyond salvation. The details show the wood dowel with top "softened" which protrudes slightly and keeps the bottom edge of the door from sagging and scraping as it closes; the handle; and the upper left corner with special hinges, straight rather than rounded along the front. Height 63 cm., width 26 cm., depth 14 cm. Oil finish. 1971.

The coffee table was designed for people who had a rather large room, and as you view it from some distance, you get an upward sweep of the legs and the taper, the way they lift up under the top of the table. There is a lightness there. At the same time, I think the table rests firmly on the floor. It's got it's own stance, a definite posture.

Doing the top as it is here, in two halves, may seem eccentric. I have done it as one whole piece glued together. But this way is more fun, really. It's kind of a smile—a joke perhaps. It may puzzle some, but for most people it's pleasant, a change from the monotony of just the solid, one-piece top.

I left a space between the two halves, the two planks that I had, which matched fairly well together. I made the opening large enough so that you could get in there with a small brush or a dustcloth, so I don't think it will irritate anyone.

The wood in the top is doussie. It ages beautifully—reddish brown, and takes a lovely finish, oiled as it is here. A finish that is easy to keep up year after year, helping the piece to grow old gracefully.

The legs and underpart are a wood called veroola that I bought in a small lumberyard. If you look in the textbooks, you won't find anything called veroola. But these old people, the foremen and workmen in little yards, have gotten such names somewhere once, and they have stuck. I like it. There is a sort of romance about the whole thing. There isn't much of any such wood around, and when some strange person like myself comes along and begins looking for it, they rather enjoy it. They get a smile out of the fact that someone is still alive who cares about these odds and ends of wood and uses them in finished pieces to make something that people enjoy, something that is a little bit different.

Coffee table of doussie.
Right: *Detail of two-piece top. Doussie wood has porous end-grain like bamboo.*
Opposite: *Full view of the coffee table, and details. The top is of doussie, the stand is veroola, a darker color red. The legs do not quite touch the top: a crosspiece partly notched into the sides supports the table top. Length 130 cm., height 60 cm., width 63 cm. Oil finish. First made in 1968.*

Next is a cabinet in pear wood. Now, right from the start I want to remind you that ordinarily pear wood—the classical pear wood we associate with furniture—is steamed pear wood, reddish in color. That is because they take the log and they saturate it with steam, which gives it a homogeneous pinkish color. The reason is that pear wood, when used in production of furniture, more than one-of-a-kind, varies so much in color that it causes a great deal of extra labor and time, which people working in furniture production are not interested in. So they steam it to make it an even color. That way they can just use it as *a* wood.

But here, now, is natural, unsteamed pear wood as it grows and as you cut it. It varies in color from log to log, and within the same plank there is a change, too. So getting this cabinet to be intentional in its tone, with the shadings the way I want them, entailed a great deal of labor.

Each plank was lighter on the outside than it was inside. I had to make additional cuts to get at the desired colored parts of wood. This odd color change occurs when a freshly cut log is sawed. Chemical changes take place during the drying process. But this is natural pear wood and it has all the charm and difficulties of working in it. It's quite an adventure to open up these planks and see what is inside.

The door panels, for example—the pattern of these panels is a great rarity because the color, the heart color of the wood, is usually in the middle of the log. And usually the log is cracked, just there, so you get very little of this red that is ever whole and usable. But here the color, beautiful as it is, has gone off on a wandering, a journey of its own toward the side of the log, and gone in spots and streaks as you see it.

This is the only time I have encountered it like this in maybe fifteen years. Among several dozens of planks of pear wood that I have had, here it is, this pattern. Only once. And it is charming. It's a thrill to work, but it's a great responsibility. I've gotten something that has just once occurred in my time as a cabinetmaker, and perhaps I never will have it again. One wrong cut, and I can spoil the whole piece.

This cabinet, too, was not drawn up or really planned. It wasn't designed in the sense that I knew from the start how it would look. Details came to me along the way. I made changes from an original rough little sketch that I had. I guessed. I worked by different stages. Try. Change. Look again.

Detail of pearwood cabinet on page 91. Drawers of secupira contrast, but do not conflict with, the soft texture of the pearwood.

I often make the doors of my cabinets first because it's much more difficult to find the wood and the inspiration for making one door or a pair of doors than it is to make the case of a cabinet. The doors are often decisive for me. If they are promising, then I have reason to continue with the cabinet. So I made these doors, and then, with their help, I decided what depth the cabinet should be. I began to wonder how the legs and underpart would be. I made up a curved leg and tried it, and it didn't fit. It just didn't belong to this cabinet.

Then I made a straight leg, and it seemed better. I changed the proportions, and gradually it began to belong more to the cabinet. And so I guessed my way along and composed the piece by stages.

The panels in the door—I didn't know from the start that I would even use them. I had imagined that I would have some other pear wood with the grain going in waves or swirls, and this would accentuate the curve of the door. I thought that this blotchy red pattern would sort of crease the door, would make it seem angular for the eye. But finally, after sawing up and trying other pear-wood panels, I sawed this wood with a great deal of worry and fear, because I didn't have any more. I made these panels and I think they are good. I was lucky.

The lighter edge being toward the middle of the cabinet is not just a guess. I did turn the panel both ways, and it turned out that with the lighter part toward the middle of the cabinet, you also accentuate the curve of its front. Whereas, if the darker part were in the middle, you would, perhaps, get a concave or a flatter effect. All these things are, you might say, a chain reaction—one event leading to the other—one discovery leading to another.

As you open the doors, you have the little drawers inside. The handles may seem too small at first. But remember: you don't want to take your whole hand and go in there and grip something large, because you probably will bump into the top piece of the cabinet. It will disturb you. It seems to me that the natural motion is to come from underneath with one or two fingers and just "pick" out the drawer. Sort of lift it a little bit and draw it out with a finger from underneath. It seems right and it feels good.

The drawer on the right side is smaller so it can be pulled out with only the right-hand door open. You don't have to open both doors to get at the first drawer. The larger drawer,

Below and opposite: *Cabinet in pearwood, detail and full view. (See also color plate, page 100). Height 130 cm., width 54 cm., depth about 30 cm. Outside is untreated, inside polished. 1971.*

on the left, is accessible when the cabinet is fully open.

One drawer is the size of stationery paper, for example, so if you have some documents or important papers that one usually has about the house, you can keep them in that drawer. The other is for odds and ends. The cabinet does not force you to have certain things in it. Yet, there is a good chance that the person who owns it will have some papers to keep near at hand—in this cabinet.

The rest may be books or porcelain or glass or silver. I don't really know. Needs vary. Often they are adjusted to the piece, instead of the other way around. It's someone wanting the piece itself, as it is, that is finally important.

But, of course, it can be otherwise. Sometimes we are agreed from the start that the whole thing is composed around a very definite idea, a request, and specific items that are to be kept in a certain way. I like that as a beginning. I like to work on objects that will be used very personally.

The relationship between the object I have made and how it is going to be used is important to me. But it is not so important that everything else becomes less important or unimportant. It's the sum total that I'm after; my craft experiences and what they will mean to others in the finished piece.

One person has said to me, "Now listen. This showcase is so nice, I enjoy it so much as is, that I don't have to have anything in it at all." That, in a way, is a compliment to the showcase as a piece. But, on the other hand, it would be rather disappointing for me if the same person said, "It's the kind of a showcase that would lose if you put something in it." I want the case and the contents to be composed in a whole, and to be pleasing to the person who has it.

Details of pearwood cabinet.
Opposite: *Lower right corner showing door and hinge and how the cabinet side fits onto the legs. It is double-notched so as not to shift.*
Left: *Inside of the pearwood cabinet. Note wooden catches for doors. Short drawer pulls fit behind shallow curve of doors.*
Below: *The "dip" of the grain in the door-frame is intentional: it enhances soft curve usually seen from slightly above.*

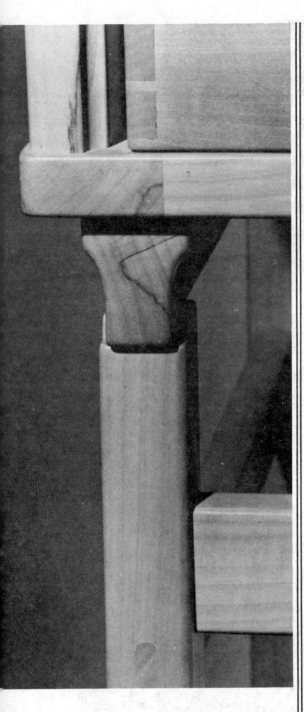

I like to make pieces which will house or contain something else that people enjoy and use. The silver chest is one of those pieces. I guess it all started when someone told me that she had nice old silver flatware but could not find any kind of cabinet or other case to hold these things in the way she wanted. People are forever having nondescript drawers lined with sprayed-in gaudy velvet or little blocks with suede covering that become soiled and dingy. There are all sorts of solutions, most of them rather makeshift and pretentious, and this disturbed my friend and it certainly always does disturb me: the contradiction between having something fine that one likes very much, and then leaving it in indifferent surroundings.

So I started to think about it, and I went to a silversmith and asked him how flatware was usually stored—in what size drawers or boxes, and how these were used. The most common fault of the storage I found was that if you have a drawer with rather heavy contents and a handle in the middle (which is customary), when you pull this drawer about two-thirds out, it starts to hang down, or it drops, and you just don't know what to do with it. You have to let go of the handle and try to grab the drawer by the two sides before it falls.

So, basic to the function of the piece was the fact that it had to be more than drawers. It was to be drawers and also trays which you could pull comfortably out of the case and then carry to a table, or (and here another idea came to me) put atop the case itself, one drawer at a time. The drawer then rests in the grooves along the sides of the top, but does not touch the polished surface itself. Then the contents of the other drawers are easily accessible.

I made a little sample part of the drawer—a side-and-front, with a little grip which later became much softer and shaped quite differently. The first trial was awkward both in form and dimensions but it confirmed the idea and so I began to do the case. I did make a drawing, but I didn't follow the drawing afterwards, not exactly. And I drew only the case itself. I thought it was going to be a piece that would be placed on a sideboard and did not think of a stand at first. It was only after I had finished the case that I realized it would do well on a stand.

The whole piece is more difficult than it looks and I can only do it when I am rested and feel strong and optimistic.

Above and opposite: Silver chest, detail and full view. Case and stand are chestnut, drawers of pearwood. The chest can be removed from its stand. A drawer can be placed between shallow grooves atop the chest, where it rests without touching the top surface itself. Height 74 cm., width 47 cm., depth 38 cm. Oiled outside, rest untreated. First done in 1961.

PLATE 1.

Upper left: *Body of the clock showing only hours and seconds. Body is of tulip-wood, hands are Macassar ebony. The choice of grain (from a half-billet of tulip wood) gives the chiseled hollow face its soft, unlined, watercolor effect. Grain forming definite lines here would only detract from the shape.*

Right: *The full clock. The stand is of veroola wood, laminated. The two forward-bent legs are made on the same asymmetric mold but one was joined to the main ("fishpole") part with its curve inverted (the one being more tense, or sharp, towards its lower end). Total height of stand is about 170 cm., diameter of clock face is about 22 cm.*

Lower left: *Jewelry box of Andaman padouk, oiled outside. The inside is untreated, and after six years it still has the spicy fragrance of this fine rare wood. The fittings are silver. Length 28 cm., width 21 cm., height 11 cm. 1969*

PLATE 2.

Upper left: *Wall cabinet in birds' eye maple, waxed outside, oil-painted inside. There was a crack on the inside of one door, and I had to decide whether to save the rare and charming wood by repairing the door—or lose it all, since such reparation can never result in a perfect, unblemished surface. I chose to repair the crack and paint the inside of the cabinet. This is the only time that I have done so. A small wood pivot-pin at bottom opens the right-hand door. Height 72 cm., width 37 cm., maximum depth 14 cm. 1972.*

Upper right: *The cabinet open. Visible handles on these very special doors would spoil them.*

Lower left: *Cabinet of Swedish yellow ash. The entire piece with its elusive, somehow deceptive shapes is the result of these particular pieces of wood arranging themselves to please—and even surpass—the cabinetmaker's hesitant intent. The doors are planed to a slight curve, though not compound-curved like barrel-staves, which the pattern of the grain would have us believe. Height 86 cm., width 47 cm., total depth 16 cm.*

Lower right: *The drawers are of African kari-wood, which is similar to doussie. The back of the cabinet is a solid wood frame-and-panel.*

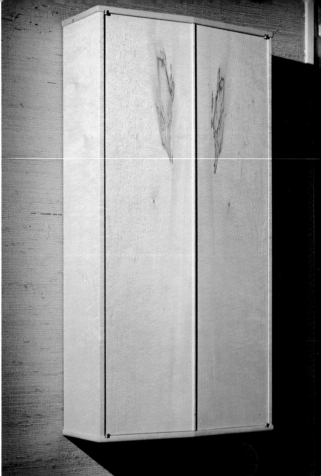
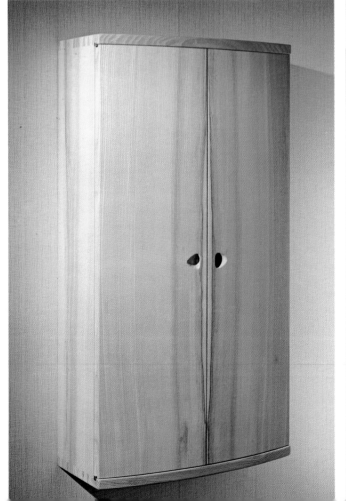

PLATE 3.

Left: *Cabinet in cherry wood: the result of one small but perfect log which I kept for years, afraid to touch for fear of spoiling it. The cabinet is oil-finished outside, with the showcase interior polished in the old, classic manner. The inside parts of the drawer are of aromatic Lebanon cedar. Height 163 cm., width 55 cm., maximum depth 26 cm.*

Upper right: *"Ballet-dancer" cabinet of English brown oak. Not imposing, it stands as if on tiptoe. The concave doors and softly rounded sides are hand-planed; most of the stand is worked with a fine spoke-shave, and the burnished wood is left unsanded. Untreated. Height 132 cm., width 41 cm., depth about 18 cm. 1972.*

Lower right: *Cabinet in lemonwood. This wood encourages fine lines and small, neat bevels: its delicacy would be lost on imposing shapes. Oiled outside, polished inside. Height 160 cm., width 67 cm., depth 23 cm.*

PLATE 4.

Upper left: *Cabinet of natural pearwood. The wood in the convex curved panels is a rarity, with its unharmed patches of the heart-color—usually this area of the wood is cracked. The texture of pearwood is exquisitely delicate to both eye and hand. Height 130 cm., width 54 cm., depth 30 cm. Untreated.*

Upper right: *The inside of the pearwood cabinet. Shelves are adjustable on carved wooden consoles with pegs. Drawer-fronts and pulls are of secupira. The one-piece panels have been carefully planed, not bent, to the shape of the door-curve.*

Below: *Coffee table. The two-part top is of doussie, the stand is veroola. Oil-finished, these hard woods wear well and age gracefully. Length 130 cm., height 60 cm., width 63 cm.*

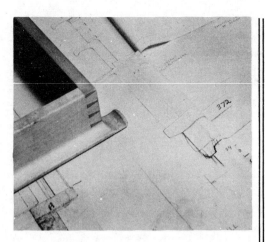

Above: *One of the few preliminary drawings I have made—for the silver chest—and the first awkward trial corner of the drawer with handle.*
Below and opposite: *Details of the silver chest. The underside of the handle is softly scooped; the entire shape of the handle must flow unspoiled into the front and sides of the drawer.*

People have come to me through the years and wanted me to make one for them, and usually I say, "Perhaps in the autumn after summer vacation, when I feel relaxed and able, I just might try it. If I have some very special wood I haven't used in it before, and know I want to try again." So over a period of twelve or thirteen years I have perhaps done six or seven of these cases and no two have been identical, because the drawing is not exact. I have no drawing at all of the stand, just a few dimensions jotted down. Besides, I do not use templates or jigs, but work by eye. Each time I shape the legs, tapering from the floor up, they are a bit different, and there is much detail work to be done on the sculptured drawers with their rather complicated construction.

The legs are especially enjoyable to do, since shaping them is perhaps the best example of using my planes (except to get a surface flat and shimmering) that I can think of. Each leg is curved slightly on the two outer sides, and all four edges are rounded. Simple enough. But here's where the fun comes in: the curve starts in slowly at the bottom, increases to a maximum about two-thirds of the way up, and then flares out near the top. I do it all with a plane; holding it at a very slight angle diagonally at first, increasing the angle at the greatest curve and then decreasing it at the top end. All in one natural movement. Natural, that is, if you can get that relationship between angle and stroke all into one motion. It has to make sense, work its way into your consciousness, and become a rhythmic motion. Once you get it, the satisfaction is for free, all yours. The same applies to the rounding: it is less at the top and bottom, greatest at the sharpest part of that curve. The two curves either work together, or you haven't done it right. I've tried doing it with a spokeshave, yes, and with a cabinet-scraper. But nothing can give me that curve as well as does one of my favorite short planes.

Everything is enjoyable as long as it goes well. But to keep it going well is a very complicated exercise in concentration. The drawers are most difficult, so usually I make them first, because there is no sense in continuing unless I have been lucky enough to make the drawers the way I want them. It is a thing I enjoy doing when I have the strength. People have appreciated it and those who have one care for it and truly use it. It fills its function very well. And each time someone says he likes it and uses it, I am as happy as I was when someone said that for the first time.

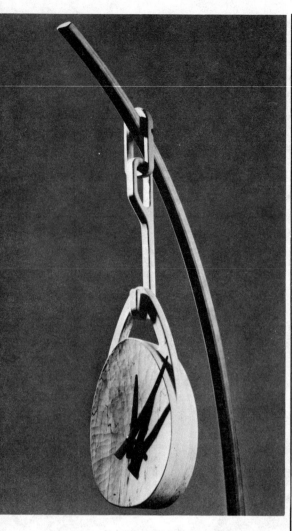

Above and opposite: *Details of the first clock. (See also color plate, page 97). The body and links are carved from one piece of spalted boxwood, the stand is of laminated cherry wood. The hands—hour and minute—are of Macassar ebony. The mechanism causes the clock to pulsate as it hangs. Total height with stand 170 cm., clock face about 20 cm. 1973.*

For years people were after me to make a clock. And I'd usually say, "Almost anybody who works in wood makes a clock or many clocks, so probably I won't do one." There was no inspiration or encouragement at all in the clocks I saw. They were usually made of odd pieces of wood that had been somehow subdued into being the background or the border of the mechanism. Or someone had burned the wood, or stained it, giving it a constructed, artificial air. There was no message in this—just a warning. So I went on making my cabinets and tables and other things.

I had among my odds and ends of wood several pieces of boxwood that I had picked up in a small yard in London near one of the canals. Piles of this boxwood had been lying out in the weather for many years. I guess it had come from Asia, and it wasn't of very large dimensions, but there was a great deal of it and it was just lying in the rain and the sun, under the London dust and grime. And cracking, of course, and being discolored by the effect of dirt and water going through it. I picked up a few pieces of this wood and took them home. However careful I was with the drying, that wood just simply cracked and cracked. I could hear these terrible little clicking sounds now and then as the wood split. Because these small trees, or large bushes, grow very slowly and turn with the seasons, the grain was in a twist and the cracks were running in spirals. So there was almost no place that I could get a fairly large straight piece. The wood just lay there in my shop.

Then one day, suddenly, I was making a clock. I don't know whether it began with the boxwood or with the idea of a very light, airy stand of bent wood. And the idea of a clock hanging . . . that was it! I took a scrap of thin, straight wood and I tied it against a post in the shop and then I tied a line on the end of it, fastened that on to the workbench, and bent this piece of wood exactly as one would a fishing pole. But it was coming straight up off the floor and then bending forward, and I didn't like the curve. So I put a block of wood between the post and the floor end of the piece, the butt of the piece. Suddenly it began making sense, because it was bending back just as a fishing pole does when you have a big one on the line and you are straining back and the pole is first bending backward and then making a long sweep forward. I began to like the curve, and then I bent some other very thin pieces for the "legs," the protruding parts, at the floor, because

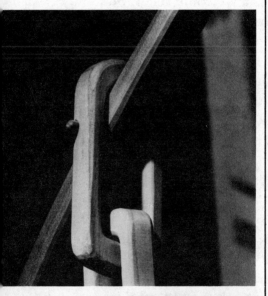

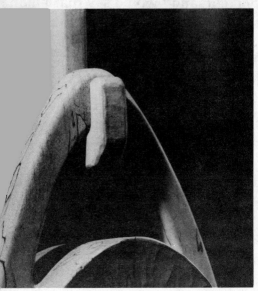

I knew it had to be a three-point arrangement. Gradually the curves emerged, and I called this whole thing "the fishing pole." I drew patterns from the curves and then started to make the clock; it was a sort of one-sweep project, you know, unbroken. I just started it and kept right on going.

The result was a surprise. On the day I finished it, I came down in the evening to look at it. I hadn't had a glass, I was cold sober, but the clock was moving: the body of the clock hanging from the "fishing pole," or stand, was throbbing! It has been throbbing ever since. Something in the action of the clock itself, and the fact that it is hanging from a carved wooden chain of several links and a hook—all these factors together made the clock pulsate. It was and is a clock with a heart.

People have noticed it. Some have found it surrealistic, others merely think it naive. It was my first clock and I kept debating with myself as to whether or not it was good. Good or bad. The question is unanswered.

A year or so went by and friends kept asking me whether I would make another clock like the first and I said, "No; if I make a clock at all it certainly won't be like that one." Not being an inventive person, I didn't know just how to come up with a new idea. If a clock is to be worth doing, it should have a distinct personality of its own. That, at least, was certain.

For a long time I just let it ride. Then another idea came to me; it happened when I was feeling relaxed. This time it wasn't a fishing pole that set me going; I already knew that I wanted something like the stand I had done for the first clock. But this was going to have quite another kind of mood— a fun thing! I had a wonderful piece of tulip wood, half a log. There were some cracks in it, though not too many; if I cut it a certain way the face would form a natural oval with the grain and would be rather interesting, not just red, but with some of the sapwood also there in a swirl. The whole thing suddenly began to take form, and appealed to me. So I made the oval of the clock, then did a good deal of sawing into parts and putting back together in order to form the opening for the works, and then I fit the back piece: a little lid which is fitted very carefully with a small bolt to lock it and enclose the mechanism.

Now came the fun part, because what drove me was the thought of a clock with only hours and seconds. So I made the hour hand, balanced it fairly well, and then shaped the

long second hand so that at six and twelve it would be flush with the outer rim of the oval. When I put the battery in and started the mechanism, it fooled me again. I was startled to find that the second hand of the clock was not just making the expected distinct jerk forward at each second, a purely mechanical movement, but was somehow *fluttering* ahead.
It would take half a movement back and then a step ahead, which gave it a very special humorous rhythm, a marvelous movement. Here was a clock—and a mobile.

Twelve and three and six and nine were points of orientation, vertical and horizontal. But there was nothing to go by: no notches, no numbers. I would stand and look at the clock and know that it was somewhere between two and ten minutes past two, and I found this a welcome relief. Suddenly I wasn't looking at my watch thinking, "My goodness, it's six minutes past two and in four minutes I have to rush down to the station and catch the train to town," or, "It is twenty minutes past three and in ten minutes I have to meet so-and-so," or meet some other deadline.

The effect of the clock was so soothing and at the same time amusing that I did not want to part with it, didn't want to sell it. I'd look at it on the way upstairs or coming down to work: the second hand with that fluttering of its own would disappear at the vertical and then gradually it would reappear at the sides of the oval and flutter and grow and then diminish and disappear at the bottom and then come fluttering up the other side with a humor all its own. My visitors and friends would stand there and get a little laugh, and relax. They would ask me why I did it, and I would say that I didn't know, maybe just because I hoped that someone would be amused by it or because at my age, some of the seriousness and grim determination had worn off and I was allowing myself to laugh at myself and my work.

I made the clock after doing a large but very exacting cabinet. Sometimes after such tense work I make myself a plane as a change of pace; this time it was a clock. Many people asked if they could buy it and for a long time I said that I could not sell it or that I would not sell it, but finally I realized that I couldn't afford to keep it. A man who already had several of my things kept asking about the clock, and now he has it. Whenever we speak on the telephone, I ask him what time it is, and he says, "Well, it's about . . ." this or that o'clock. And we laugh together.

Opposite: *Clock #2—just hours and seconds. Body of tulipwood with hands of ebony. Stand and connecting yoke of veroola. The middle photo shows the flutter of the second hand in motion and that the back of the case can be opened to provide access to the mechanism. Height of stand 175 cm., clock face about 22 cm., maximum diameter.*

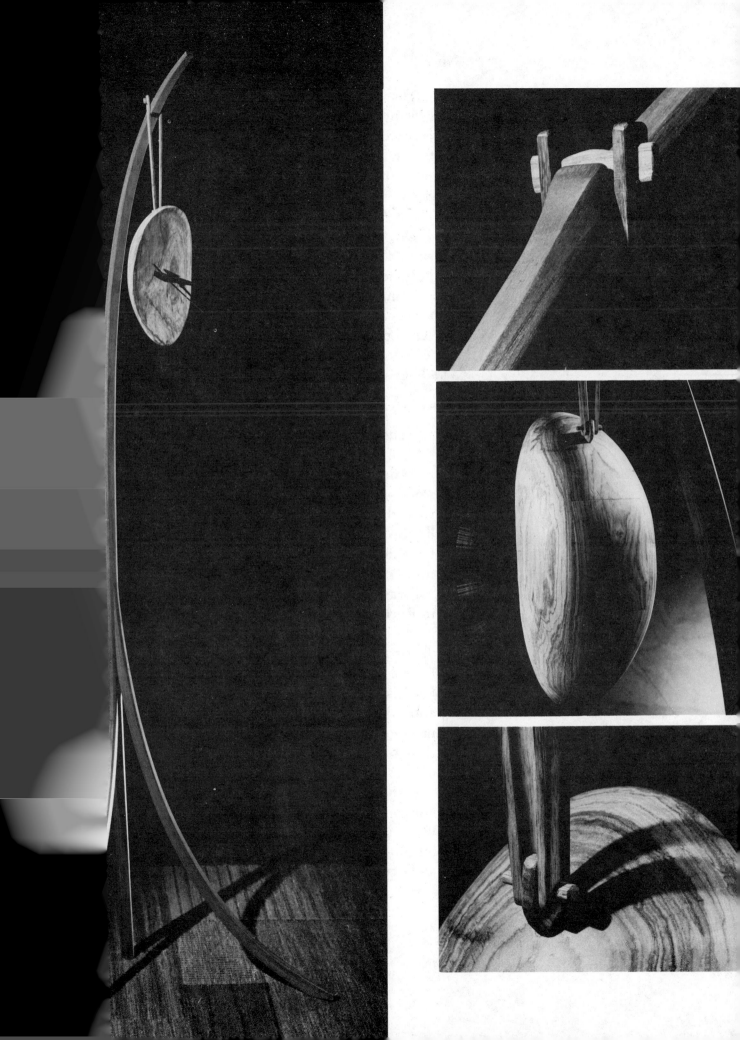

These are some aspects of my work. It is not a work of certainty, but a work of chance, of hoping and seeking, and it is work in a wonderful material—a rich material about which we have forgotten a great deal. We take a lot for granted when it comes to wood. We tend towards generalities. We become almost nonchalant about the material itself, and just think, "Well, it's a material. Someone has used it."

One can "use" it. But one can also listen to it. Perhaps we should think more about wood as being specific, alive, and very demanding. There are who knows how many different personalities of just maple wood. That is to say, maple wood varies from tree to tree, just as one person varies from another person. No two people are identical. No two trees are identical. No two planks are identical, and this is the first joy of working.

You get the impulse from the very texture and rhythm and color and feel of a particular wood, a particular plank, a particular piece of it. This entails a great effort and a good deal of luck.

And it's not being done everywhere in the world. Maybe, sometimes, I feel like a bit of an anachronism, out of step with the times. I don't know. At any rate people are amused by the fact that someone is still around doing this. In fact, I am told I am one of the few people who has the tenacity to go on working this way.

I was asked to teach at the School for American Craftsmen in Rochester, New York, and encourage young people to be just a little less dramatic and less sensational in their work. To be a bit more patient and careful and a good deal more humble. And this I did, and enjoyed doing it because I have friends in the United States, just as I have friends in Japan, and in England, and elsewhere. It is extremely gratifying to me to work for people and among people and find that the things that I do mean something to someone, somewhere, in these truly strange and hurried times.

Perhaps the very main reason that I'm still energetic and still working as a craftsman is just this sense of contact with wood, contact with people, and a quality that, even if it is a bit out of step with the times, somehow manages to survive and even gain appreciation.

"HOW DO YOU HAPPEN TO BE WORKING WITH WOOD; how did you become a cabinetmaker?" The question used to surprise me a little because I have never really been aware of any definite point when I began to work with wood; it has always been there for me.

My parents were Russian. Life as it was in their youth allowed them many pleasures—long visits abroad, the finest education, leisure, art. They were adventurous: on an "amateur" expedition they crossed all of Russia, the mountains, the Taiga, great rivers in Siberia, making a journey that took over a year. They went all the way to Petropavlovsk. This was around 1919, an uneasy time. During a conversation with the Governor, my mother said, "I would like to do something—to be useful." Useful! She who had hardly seen the kitchen of her sumptuous home. "Ah, yes," the Governor said, "we are opening a school. It's on the edge of the world. But who'd want to go there?" "I would," said my mother. She and my father did go, and they lived and taught for three years among the Chukchis in a village called Uelen on the Arctic Circle. I was born there.

That place on the Chukotsk Peninsula was undoubtedly the happiest period of my mother's long and unusual life. She moved from her sable and brocade, her Fabergé jewelry, from her governess and boarding-school background, to a schoolhouse where water had to be melted from snow and wooden floors scrubbed by hand. Mother loved Uelen, and the Chukchis simply adored her. She learned the language, became a part of the life. Everything was unspoiled—as it had been for ages. Before my parents left Uelen, the Chukchis gave Mother a collection of miniature ethnic items, the most exquisite objects—little sleds and tiny clothing and carved dancing figures, a large ceremonial drum. Wood and ivory, sealskin and sinew, each piece simple perfection. Few museums have anything like these treasures, once my playthings. All are long since gone, except a yellowed album which is still around. And maybe one thing more survives: the sense that between the very primitive and the most refined there is some sort of basic affinity that transcends values, links everything together. Metaphysics? Maybe.

After Uelen we moved to Shanghai, where I had a grandfather; two years later we went to the United States, to Seattle. The Depression was coming, but my parents managed to get work teaching in Alaska, far into the interior, on the

Kuskokwim River, which is the second largest river in that wilderness. From these years I have recollections of my own. remember the few log cabins and the schoolhouse that wer the village called Sleetmute, on the banks of the great, slow moving river. The Indians made fine-lined canoes, wooden sleds, snowshoes which they carved with knives fashioned ou of the bent parts of steel fox traps. They would make these curved knives, and then sit in their overheated cabins, workin during long winter evenings, coughing ominously, slowly carving various utensils and snowshoes.

My father was an outdoor man. He loved hunting and fish ing, and he made knives out of files which he heated, forged t shape, and retempered. He had rifles—all sorts of guns—or pegs along the wall, among them an old 404 elephant gun. 404—in Alaska! He'd polish the wooden gunstocks, put a dro or two of oil on his hand, and then rub and rub the dark walnu He never tired. Some of the guns he never used, but the stoc of each was truly beautiful, satiny and with a deep luster.

The natives told us legends in broken English which Mothe faithfully wrote down; naive, ancient tales of the first peopl about spirits that rode the winds or assumed the shape of recognizable objects or implements, about the wolverine an the bear and the fox. We read legends of the North as so muc fiction today, but to a boy in the midst of it, fifty years ago, was not all fiction—not quite.

Many of the natives had tuberculosis, and each year one o more died. Mother buried them in a little churchyard beside th small, almost forgotten log church with its Russian icons.

One spring we had a sudden flood. The ice jammed on a island just below the river, and in a few hours the water rose u to the eaves of the cabins. We spent three days floating amon the cabins in boats full of grownups, children, and howling malamute dogs. Some of the wooden crosses in the graveyar broke loose in the water and floated up. The natives, who wer very superstitious, took this for a bad omen. Still, the ice jam i the river did break, and the flood passed.

The year after the flood, a forest fire nearly wiped out th village. In those days there were no forest rangers, airplane or protection of any kind. This fire started through the car lessness of a native berry-picker; it grew into one of those ur controlled crown fires, and curled right up to the village. Da and night the people had to back-fire and dig trenches aroun the settlement to save the houses.

About 1928 we left Sleetmute, going 450 miles down the river on an old sternwheeler steamboat. Two years later we were back "up north," this time in southeastern Alaska on Cook Inlet, at a village called Tyonek. Cook Inlet was a place of extremely high tides and many storms. The tides were said to be the second highest in the world; in the autumn they were thirty-four feet. The water would rise and fall, surge and recede. There was a long sloping beach, and during storms the waves would crash up the shore and then roll back, and you would get the sound of the pebbles and stones rolling together with the water. There were agates and a lot of low-grade coal which the water would undermine and break from the bank. Pieces of this coal would be rolled among the stones into something like briquettes; the whole beach was blackish pieces of coal and rough agates speckling the slope of gray that crunched under one's feet.

A lot of bark drifted in; I'd get pieces of it and carve simple little model sailboats for myself, boats that I sailed along the creek that ran behind the village. I must have been about nine or ten years old at the time. I always had a knife with me, and often my little .22 rifle. I was a rather good hunter—in a place where there were snipe and ducks in the nearby marshes, and in wintertime, ptarmigan, hard to see in the snow. Winter and summer I made things for myself: boats, little carvings, bows and arrows. Sometimes I played with the Indian children—if and when they showed up. "I will play with you yesterday," they'd say, and then forget.

After three and a half years we left Tyonek and went back to Seattle. Seattle is where I grew up; I lived there until I went to Europe. My parents separated, and I lived with my mother in a small cottage on the beach near a lighthouse. Alki Point. A magic place, right on the shore. Our little garden sloped down toward the sea and a breakwater; when the tide was high, the waves would thud against it.

This was the Depression; Mother was on the W.P.A., the government program for the unemployed. She found the cottage and thought it would be a good place for me to grow up. The rent was twenty-five dollars a month, which no doubt was half of what she earned. Yet she managed to get a small Indian hair rug for the tiny livingroom, and in a pawnshop she found two Oriental chairs. They were really strange. I remember them still—ornate, dark wood, gold brocade seats. Just before she bought them she said to me, "I really don't dare do this." She was counting pennies. She'd save, then go downtown to see if the chairs were still there. Some diplomat who had been stationed in the Far East had brought them out with him and then left them in the pawnshop where Mother caught sight of them. She had an eye for beauty, the unusual, things that were fascinating. So we got the chairs. From somewhere there came curtains, richly embroidered in faded soft wool, and an Italian lantern, one of those lanterns intended for a candle. It was in delicate curves with the bent iron in a sort of filigree.

We lived in our little cottage and were very poor. But we did have a radio; there was always fine music. And we had a fireplace for which we got sacks of bark that floated in on the beach, bark that smelled of forest, seasalt, and the oil that was always in the water. The ships gliding by would pump out water, a lot of which had oil in it. There would be this wonderful smell, warmth, and music. After a storm, the sun shone through salt-speckled windows. And there were these lovely things.

The front lawn of our cottage was really mostly weeds and a few wildflowers, ending in the breakwater. The water was salt, the air was salt, and there were mountains around, and always boats and ships on the Sound. I had school comrades along the beach who lived in various houses between me and the lighthouse at Alki Point. We visited one another and we got to building boats together. We'd work in a basement (one or two of the boys lived in houses large enough to have a basement), and these basements were always open and we came and went and worked on our boats and chatted about sailing and books about the sea. We could hear the lighthouse when there was fog—five on and five off; on a foggy night there would be the flash of the light and then the horn would sound that deep o-o-o-o in the thick darkness. Sometimes we could hear the propeller of a big ship in ballast going by the Point. We used to even try to guess what ship it was by the sound of the engine and the thud—one, two, three, four; one, two, three, four—of the propeller.

On the way to my friend's, strolling along the beach, I always passed the house of Captain Coffin. His name was Everett Coffin, and he was an old sea captain from Nantucket. As you approached his house, you saw the storm door of canvas, and on the canvas was painted a full-rigger in a very bad storm, reefed down. I think the old man had done the painting himself, and it was charming and impressive. Beside the steps of the house there was a dory resting on chocks and a wooden cradle he had built. Over the dory was a neat canvas cover that he had sewn himself and then treated with oil so that it would be waterproof. I don't remember really how I met the old man the first time, but gradually we became good friends.

I was building boats, and he used to advise me about them and sometimes—not very often—but sometimes when the weather was good and there was no mud on the road, he would invite me in to see some of the things that he had in his living room. I was invited on days when it hadn't rained because then my feet were not muddy. Captain Coffin's wife, Laura, was a very strict woman, and she kept their house spic and span. And she kept a very strong and watchful eye over Everett because he used to like to go down on the beach and gather all sorts of odds and ends that floated in—planks and bits of wreckage and gear from old ships. Through his acquaintances and friends along the waterfront, he would acquire an old block, tarred line, turnbuckles; anything from ships or boats. Everett loved to go down on the beach during a storm, and gather up whatever the waves offered. He would get his hands dirty and maybe his shoes, and Laura was always there to scold him about that and tell him to take off his shoes before he came into the house. He had to walk through the kitchen. He didn't use the front door; the living room was carpeted, and he had to wash up before he could come in there.

In his living room were photographs of, oh, all sorts of vessels; mostly his former commands or ships that he had met in his long life at sea and that appealed particularly to him. He had a clock—one of those wonderful old grandfather clocks with the moon and the months and days and such on it that tick-tocked there in the room; that clock had come with him around the Horn in one of his first commands. Also, an album with all sorts of fascinating photographs. He would sit and show these things to me and we'd talk about sheer and flare, bowspirits that were beautiful and bowspirits that were not charming or beautiful at all, the rigging and spars in particular types of ships, and how the sterns were formed, sometimes gracefully rounded, elegantly sculptured, and sometimes abruptly cut off square and not interesting at all, and he'd tell me about how everything on a ship had its purpose; the way it all came about was a story in itself—the way each thing was shaped, the way it was used.

We used to sit for hours like that, and he told me he had

been in whalers out of New Bedford and had made voyages of sometimes one or two or even three years. He explained to me about the wonderful whale boats that they had on these ships. The boats with which they hunted the whales were lightly planked and beautifully shaped, and they were flexible and rode the waves. If they had been brittle, if they had been more heavily built, they would probably have been shattered by the seas, but because they were supple and light, they were marvelous sea boats. I made for him a model of a whale boat which was about fourteen inches long, as well as I could in every detail, and I think that it was fairly well done because the captain was a very honest and sincere man and he looked at the model and he nodded approval and he had it there in his home for many years.

Beside his storm door there was a ship's bell. This was the bell from the old steamer *Tacoma*, which was Captain Coffin's last command. They had given him the ship's bell and he had mounted it on his house. Sometimes when I sailed by, he'd open the door, come out, and sound that bell. There was an aura about the old man, and not only romance, but also some kind of a mystical purpose, logic, in what he told me and in things we saw together.

I sailed a lot in the small boats that I built, sailed alone most of the time, but also with my comrades. Each in our own boat, we'd sail across Puget Sound to a cove and an abandoned harbor called Port Blakely. At that time, around 1937–38, there were some old schooners laid up there—the awkward type of schooner that they used in the lumber trade and the coal trade. They were quite abandoned and stripped of almost everything. We used to climb aboard a ship and sometimes go down into the murky hold where there was still some moldy canvas, old sails and the like. We went into the cabin aft, and once I found a ditty bag there. In it were a sailors' palm and some rusty needles. On the bag you could still see the stenciled name, *Commodore*. I took that bag and cleaned it up and got some marlin, a palm, and other things and had it in my boat.

Still in my memory are those old ships and weathered wood everything on a heavy, ponderous scale. Sometimes I have wished that I could work in wood in a big, powerful scale, but it is not in me. I'm a person who works rather meticulously, does selected delicate objects, and if I try to do something powerful it doesn't come off well. You might ask if I am prejudiced against large-scale things. I am not—as long as they are not awkward and badly done. I admire heavy work, well-built houses, something timbered, sculptures that have a power about them. But I cannot do it myself. Nor can I teach it to others.

Later on, after we had lived in Seattle for maybe ten years, I worked in a small shipyard on Lake Union. It was owned by a Danish family and we had many fine yachts there. They were wood, of course; this was before the time of plastics. We had charge of hauling these boats out in wintertime and keeping them and then fitting them out in the spring: painting, rigging, everything. There were old but still sleek six-meter yachts built in Norway and Sweden and Denmark which had once raced for the Gold Cup, and other beautiful sailing boats. Also we had one of the most famous ocean racers of all times, the *Dorade*. She was a fairly old boat but a grand little ship, and she had aged gracefully. We'd haul her up on the slip, and the young son of the owner of the shipyard would stand there and look at her from below, look at the lines of that boat, and he would just shake his head and say, "Boy, she sure has got sex appeal!" And she did!

Probably I talk too much about ships, but they had a definite and lasting effect upon me, with their grace or lack of grace, their symmetry—not that perfect symmetry, but always something alive. And, of course, whatever one may say, some of that is gone now. We have aerodynamics and the exactness of nylon rather than the romance of Egyptian cotton, and nylon line rather than tarred hemp. Some of the yachts today are much faster. But they just don't have that romantic appeal for people like myself, so perhaps there is something to regret. It was the straight line that was not quite straight; it was just enough strain by intent and by use to be alive, to have a message for whoever understood. Nowadays some of us miss this and are turning back, but we are looking at it at a distance. We can't quite return to the obvious and proper place that much of this had in our lives. Attempts to go back are usually doomed to fail for various reasons—different materials, new and different skills, a different life. But whatever it was in the past, a lot of it rubbed off and I have it still and I am very happy that I do have it.

Sailing alone, I was never lonely. We boys had great times. In the evening we built fires on the beach with driftwood that smelled of creosote, with bark and pieces of old logs or boxes. The lighthouse would blink and four of us who were great buddies would sit there and watch the ships, talk about the sea and about the larger yacht that we were going to build and sail far—certainly around the world. I even had a well-known naval architect by the name of Ralph Winslow draw the plans, designs that cost a good deal; I had them with me for years. The war came and we were scattered. The boat was never built, and the plans are somewhere left behind.

I read Conrad, of course, his *Youth*; the *Judea* of London reminded me somehow of the *Commodore*. I think the *Judea* met a more worthy, a more dignified, fate than the old schooner rotting away in Blakely Harbor. Then I read many of Masefield's books—*Victorious Troy*, and others. But the book which has made the deepest impression on me is Saint-Exupéry's *Wind, Sand and Stars*. I don't know how many times I have returned to it; it is an addition to one's life. It has been about thirty-five years since I got the book, and I still have it, with fingerprints on it, an aura around it, notes in the margins. Now and then I return to it, not just reading it as a book but to relive a paragraph or a sentence or two. Everything is still there.

The war over, it was inevitable that I should go to Europe; I come from a family of restless people. Friends told me that in Sweden one could easily find work. And I did find work as soon as I got there. It was piecework, in industry, in factories where we made electrical equipment, radios, and neon-light fixtures. One was under a great deal of pressure and had use for dexterity and endurance. But I earned a lot. In fact I earned so much that the motion-study man at the factory used to shake his head.

At the end of each winter I had saved up enough money to take a princely vacation, to say that I would leave for a month or two and be back in the fall. With the shortage of labor in Sweden, I knew that in the autumn I could return to the same factory or find other work. So several times, alone, I went to the mountains way up in the north of Sweden, those mountains with their great distances and indescribable light—the softness of the light, the old, soft light of snow lingering in the summer mountains! The mountains are not jagged like the European peaks, but polished by ice, glaciers, and somehow mellowed by the light of countless centuries. The moss was soft under my feet, and I walked and walked and met no one, and yet there was always a presence around—the birds and the lemmings and the fish in the streams. There were reindeer on the crests of the hills grazing on the snowy slopes where it's cool in the summertime and they could get away from the flies and mosquitoes. Now and then I came to an abandoned peasant's hut, a summer pasture-place, one or two log cabins with sod roofs. There were small birches or other trees sprouting from the moss and the sod of the roofs, and I would stay a day or two or three in one of these little huts and then tell the people in the village that I was there. They were curious. They would nod and smile and let me stay as long as I wanted to. Once I spent seventy days in a little cabin like that by a mountain stream. I was never lonely; it was one of the most enriching and wonderful experiences of my life.

After a few summers I knew a large area of that part of northern Sweden. I knew where there were places one could seek shelter if the weather was bad; where there were fish; where I could meet reindeer herders who, even if they were not my friends in the sense of sharing an occupation, were friendly and understanding of anyone who walked as I did and told them about other experiences that were, even across a great distance, familiar to these people who also belonged in open spaces and knew how to live alone.

I also went to France and traveled a bit there, hitchhiking and walking. This was a time when there were fewer roads and certainly fewer automobiles, and it was a good way to see the country. I went to France a second time, lazed around under the bridges, walked the streets of Paris, and made some friends. One day a young woman who had borrowed a book from another person, who in turn had borrowed it from me, wanted to return it, and we walked together and talked; the next day she was to leave for Stockholm. She left, and I lost her address. About a year went by. Walking along one of the main streets in Stockholm, I heard a voice, "Hello there!" I turned, and there she was. And she has been with me ever since.

There were many foreigners, refugees, working in Sweden (this was just after the war): Poles, Czechs, Hungarians, Rumanians, Italians. A lot of them, especially the Poles and the Czechs, were waiting for immigration visas to the United States, the land of promise. Every factory, every place of employment, was a melting pot. There were peasants, professors, doctors, and common thieves, all sorts of people. In a sense they grouped off by nationalities, and yet they didn't at all, because we were sharing the work and there was a camaraderie that transcended the petty little rivalries and touches of nationalism or exaggerated patriotism. There was a spirit; we were all in there to beat the game, to work as much as possible, earn as much as possible, save up, and then go to a better place. These people came from concentration camps, horrors. Some of them were alone, others had relatives who were—somewhere. But they were not gloomy, dark, or depressing: there was a great deal of humor and hope. It was a memorable experience.

Working in a factory was, however, killing work—the pace, the atmosphere, the lighting, everything—and I knew that I had to get out of there. But I had no idea how. Then by chance I saw in a store window some furniture that looked unusual. It was unpretentious and of nice wood. I went in and looked closer and ran my hand along the pieces and asked about them, and the more I looked, the better they felt.

This was the store and the furniture of Carl Malmsten, the grand old man of Swedish contemporary furniture. He had a school for cabinetmakers. I met the old man, and he wanted to know if I would smoke a thin cigar. I didn't, but he did. He sat there puffing, smiling that enigmatic smile of his. White-haired, he was a very dry, wiry person, with a constant squint. We talked. He wasn't sure that I would be allowed to enter his school, but the thought of having a few foreigners there appealed to him, more as a touch of additional color, as a decoration perhaps, than as a sign of his confidence in them. Finally I went to the school itself and talked to the teacher in charge, a famous guitar maker by the name of Georg Bolin. He suggested that I hang around, and after a few weeks I found myself accepted.

It was by European standards a good school, which would make it a good school by any standards. It was a traditional school, where you learned the basics of furniture and how to use certain rather simple machines; you gained a fair realization of what a chair or a table or a cabinet looked like and how they were put together. The old man had succeeded when he was very young. He came along at an opportune time, when there was a need in Sweden for an interpretation of European period furniture, classical furniture, and he was mainly responsible for a renewal or for a more contemporary view of Swedish peasant art. He designed a long series of furniture which was put into limited production. He became a household word in Sweden; with Malmsten furniture in your home, you could not be really wrong in your choice.

A lot of it was good furniture. Most of it was quite well made. But I find looking back now that much of it was overdecorated, a bit pompous, and exaggerated. And some of it, the part that came from the Swedish art, was awkward. It was not an attempt at grace, though it was essentially well thought through and well made.

From the school I got a sense of soundness in construction and basic efficiency in the use of equipment. What came later, my own discoveries and the course that I took in my work, really had very little to do with the school, which simply gave me a footing other than boats on which to continue my work with wood. Because Malmsten was extremely autocratic, I learned one other thing: that one should not be bound, limited, and categoric in one's concept of furniture. He was a patriarch, of course, and he had an absolute and biased opinion of what was a good chair or a good cabinet or a good salad bowl, or whatever. His concept was law in the school. Very few people survived the school, by which I mean remained whole in their personality and in their approach to the craft. I had the advantage of being the oldest student there at the time, and managed somehow to preserve my independence.

Still, I am grateful for the two years or so that I spent there. A lot of it was frustration, of course, but much was fun, too. We had a Spaniard there, Ramón, from Barcelona, and he knew all about how furniture should be made—how it had been done a hundred or two hundred years ago: the fine points, the tools, the techniques, how the old masters did it. He used to tell us about it, and he would cook hot Spanish food on a plate during lunch hour and the whole shop would be filled with the aroma of spices and the food that he was preparing, and he played the guitar rather well.

But when it came to cabinetmaking . . . Ramón would start with great enthusiasm with the working drawings for one of the old man's rather intricate pieces in dark, rich wood, with perhaps some marquetry or carving in it. After a day or two, he would be going into the machine room with pieces of wood, and he wasn't smiling anymore. There were furrows on his brow. Then he would come out and he would perhaps hide a piece of wood or two under his bench or in a corner, and he would get some other pieces and go into the machine room again. This time he would come out even more unhappy. He wasn't talking much now about his work. He was still cooking hot food, but the mood was not quite the same.

119

Above: *The only drawing made for the Tasmanian blackwood cabinet shown opposite.*
Below: *Detail of the cabinet—the lower righthand corner. The stand follows the curves of the cabinet case, and is about one-half inch wider than case itself to avoid a feeling of "narrowing" towards the floor.*

What happened was that he was making small mistakes, and in trying to correct one mistake, he would make a second mistake, and then he would try to correct those two mistakes and maybe make a third, and by then he had spoiled one or two important pieces of wood and was more and more depressed. He just simply did not have the—I don't know what you would call it—not exactly the intuition, let's say the logic, the combination of logic and concentration and self-confidence that it takes to keep work of that kind flowing, partly because it is very exact work with the machines in the preparatory stages and later on it is the skill of the fingers and the hand tools. If you make mistakes in the initial stages—a millimeter suddenly becoming two millimeters or three, and a right angle being something less or more than a right angle—these little mistakes follow you all through the process of work. If you are conscientious and hopeful and really want to do fine work, then it is tremendously discouraging, heartbreaking, to find that you don't have that logic, the ability to coordinate all these things.

So Ramón's knowledge of the history of furniture and the old masters and how it was done and the fine points of tools and woods really didn't help all that much. After school, which he did manage through sheer endurance and perseverance to complete, he found himself making models for city planners, cardboard and plastic models of cities of the future or replanning of cities, and then after several more years he met someone very nice from Chile and they went to Chile, where he is living now, somewhere in the mountains. He used to climb the high peaks near Barcelona. During the war he was a guide for refugees through the mountain passes of the Pyrenees, so he knew and loved mountains, and I hope he is happy because he was a sincere and warm-hearted person and he really suffered trying to do that perfect piece of furniture.

Opposite: *Showcase cabinet in Tasmanian blackwood. The color is a rich brownish-red. Height 145 cm., maximum width 84 cm., maximum depth 21 cm. The inward front curve is about 4 cm. Oil-finished to a luster outside, polished inside.*

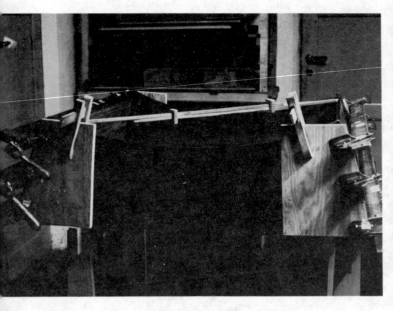

Details of working on showcase cabinet in Tasmanian blackwood: glue-ing up the carcase; selecting wood for and then shaping the one-piece front of the stand.

Detail of the "arch" in place. Observe how the grain in the bottom piece of the curved door also has a gentle upward curve.

THE STUDENTS AND I TALK ABOUT WOOD. THERE
will be the beginning of a piece of furniture not yet glued up—
maybe the first idea, pieces of wood yet to be given a final
meaning. We play with these, move them this way and that to
discover what happens as we shift the colors, lines, textures.
What happens if the lighter part of a cabinet side is against the
wall, or the dark? How does a shape or proportion change as we
move past it in a room? Certain shadings and lines add to the
pleasant curve of a convex door; others are equally important
to a concave one. Observe the graphics of wood; develop the
habit of being aware almost without thinking.

We are discovering the language of wood, which is the
language of our craft. And just as with the best of our tools,
when they become more than tools and turn into instruments
tuned to our innermost intentions, so with wood: one
discovery leads to another and another. Each hardly noticed,
seemingly small, and yet finally a part of the whole—which is
your wholeness as you work. You train your eyes to see wood,
really see it. The way you use tools may not be according to the
books; rather it is the way your hands and body move when the
work goes well that is the final interpretation of any
knowledge. You are training still another part of you, perhaps
the most important part of all—the center of you which pulls
it all together and gives it your meaning.

Learn, and enjoy it. Find out what interests you most, and
learn even more about that. Books are *not* enough: they tend
to be rigid; the intuitive person must remain flexible. Rules can
be right on paper but wrong in wood. It is usual both in craft
education and elsewhere to dwell upon design. You're told to
learn drawing, to predict shapes and pinpoint function. That's
all right for those who are put together that way. But for
others, design—drawing, projecting, predicting—is often at
the expense of feeling, of going about it in our own way. Some
people just are not the A,B,C sort: they have their own
peculiarities with the alphabet. They do get it together,
though; in words, sentences, and even poems—their way.

You've got to be able to do it while being yourself, always.
Skill is doing things so well they seem simple. Like planing by
hand the edges of two pieces of hardwood and then pressing
them together in a perfect fit, using hide glue and only the
pressure of your hands as you rub the pieces together in a tight,
permanent fit. With other glue you may clamp them, but only
lightly. No strain, no distortion, no disharmony: the fit comes

easy, with the minimum of effort. Easy . . . and yet, the human body being what it is, not so easy. The wood is very hard maple, the iron begins to dull, you press harder as you plane—and everything begins to twist. That's when you take ten minutes to sharpen the iron. Then—swish—and you've done it.

There used to be a contest for cabinetmakers, held in Copenhagen; some of the best were invited. They did all sorts of high-level professional things: classic exercises, fancy drawers with rounded *inside* corners, very special joints somewhat like the ones Peder Moos was famous for. He did a chair for a person somewhere in the Orient (so the story goes) and sent the piece by ocean freight. It was being unloaded from the ship when an elephant stepped on it. All that was left intact were the joints: the rest was smashed to splinters.

The contests were friendly but keen, not always up to date, perhaps; certainly not a public event, but with a great deal of tradition and enduring knowledge. Alas, that kind of knowhow is almost forgotten today. Though we could use most of it, a few of us at least miss the subtleties, the fine personal touches combined with the integrity of the craft. That's what most of it is about—integrity.

Wood has its integrity, elusive but definable. Wood is vulnerable; it can be spoiled by a single wrong movement of the tool. It has its textures, luster, rhythms—but only the patient hand and seeing eye can coax these forth. Never inert, wood has a will of its own, the seasonal breathing of which can split rocks and burst walls.

These are some facts of wood. For the most part we deliberately ignore them; truly, wood is an exploited and maltreated material. How else can one explain the piling up of wood into weird or slick forms, the often unbeautiful bending, the smearing on of chemicals to "protect," or prevent from drying, or to give a "deeper color." So much of our contemporary work lacks the essence of wood, as it does the essence of an understanding person. Most of what we get is in the current idiom of wood: the arty sculptural or the intricately engineered. Oh, and there's one more novelty—the folksy democratic thing. Craft in villages, in barns, in old mills. Workshops in national parks where people can see the craftsmen instead of the squirrels. What is so democratic about all this when the result is mediocre? What's the final purpose of a sculptured object in wood whose curves are meant to be experienced by eye and hand, when after a year or two the glue joints are lines with sharp, irritating edges? Where is the message of all these designed-and-engineered pieces with their uniform roundings, sanded surfaces, and calculated coolness?

No wonder our young craftsman is worried even before his practical education is complete. Anyone a bit out of step, with something special inside, is worried. It's like knowing that the better the work you do, the less your chances of living by it.

You stand there with your skill, patience, and something even more unique—and you feel alone. It is a critical point in your life; you are afraid, yet you want to go ahead and do it. But how? Certainly the odds are against you. Most of the critics—cocktail glass in one hand and sharp pencil in the other—are concerned with other things: art, trends, "forms," marketing. Most of them wouldn't recognize a low-tone, subtle, and warm piece of wood if they saw it. People will buy second- and third-hand imitations, the current overstatement, the by-the-roadside charming. They don't want your quiet, out-of-place message. They are not prepared for it because that sort of thing belies their whole way of living.

Maybe the best you can do is to accept your situation—and then defy it—if you are the kind of person who can do both. If you love wood, listen to it. Don't tell it what it must do; listen to what it wants. Work with it from inside, inside it and inside you. Be self-critical. Something has to tell you whether you have—or will have—what it takes to go all the way, against all odds, and make this your life.

Sometimes the best decision one can make is to turn aside, say "No, I can't go far enough; I'm not that good and I won't be that good, ever." There are things some of us simply can not do, even if our life depends upon it. Give me a piece of clay, put a pistol to my head, and say, "Make a rabbit!" and I'll have to say, "Shoot and be damned!" So you work with wood as a hobby, and it is a nice hobby, really. You have another job to earn money—and then putter with wood to enjoy it. But you do not earn your living doing bad things in wood.

There is at present a tendency to depict craftsmen as "let's-work-and-sing-together" people. Something like the Seven Dwarfs. But most good craftsmen work by themselves, doing all their own work. So, if you are a loner, you and your work are different from most. Accept that, and be glad. Either you are the competitive, speculating sort, or you're not. And if you aren't, then turn this fact into an asset; it can be the greatest asset of all. Realizing it helps you to stop being afraid, and allows you to be proud of living with what you do best. People will tell you that the guy up the street will make such-and-such a piece for fifty bucks. You say, "If that is what you want, *please* go to him. I would have to do it differently." Actually, you would not want to do it at all. Partly because you are not a fifty-dollar craftsman. But also because you are not a fifty-dollar person.

Stick to what you believe in; go into the work and listen. Forget about competition. Find a pace and a balance that make sense out of long hours. Try to reach the level where there is no competitor except excellence itself. "Man lives by his excellence," a fine artist and good friend of mine once said.

Can one do it? Maybe. Someone, hopefully *some*, will prove it, in a medium where appreciation is almost in inverse proportion to quality. But, then, the better the work you do, the fewer pieces you make; your work balances on an edge of integrity. Then you no longer need a hundred clients a year to keep you busy (like the guy up the street), but only ten or fifteen. It may just be possible to find them.

Tell them about wood, and how objects can grow out of an idea and a feeling. About how some things are meant to last, wear well, age gracefully—while others are not. At first people will be puzzled. But gradually those who should respond will do so. They will begin to understand. Out of understanding comes appreciation. And out of appreciation will come a basis for the evaluation which you've got to have, finally, besides the kind words.

The problem of pricing one's work is always part of our early fears. In the beginning at least, most of us are hardly in a position to determine the value of what we are doing—and we are too involved in it to measure its worth. We hope the day will come when we can do so fairly, and survive. But in the beginning we live mostly on hope. And maybe that is a good way to start: hoping, and letting the pieces gradually determine the answer by achieving their own level of appreciation.

To the question, "But how does one live meanwhile?" there is no single answer: probably according to the pattern of what your life is meant to be. Certainly nowadays men help women and women help men in a new and simple way; living has its turns and becomes the better for these.

There is a sign of change in the offing. A few young craftsmen with more than mere curiosity for wood are on the way, flitch-cutting logs and even building sheds in which to dry them. They will need help, and not just from friends. Craft critics could try to be half as arty and twice as informed about wood. Gallery owners might begin to search for unobtrusive craftsmen with a soft and friendly message. People on craft-show juries could look more closely at the unshowy, instead of yawning. Magazines could write about our craft from within, rather than on the glossy surface. Museums could use the best of what is being done, regardless of names and trends, to really inform people and give them pleasure; thus proving that whether or not such workmanship is "democratic" or valid depends upon how it is handled by those responsible enough to know its worth and generous enough to share it. We could worry less about craft groups, and more about the few persons with something important to say as craftsmen.

I have taught in America several times, and now, at the end of these reflections, I find myself still experiencing hopes—and disappointments—more intensely in this country than anywhere else. Disappointments because when it comes to wood and furniture, the superficiality in the United States is frightening, even among educators. It is so difficult to find the way to teach recognition of the richness and the integrity of wood in relation to honest, simple work. One way might be to encourage an exchange between America and Europe: the one has the energy, optimism, and curiosity—the other has tradition and a bit more patience (but also complacency and the need for renewed experience). I have tried to coax forth such an exchange on a generous and specific ground—but the effort is too much for any single person. Still, interest is growing. There is some hope today, in both places. Wood at its best remains to be discovered—and quietly enjoyed. The sheer exhaustion of skipping along the surface, of buying, buying, hurrying towards those recognizable bright things—all this may bring with it a need (if ever so slight) to slow down, look around, and listen.

"Pagoda" cabinet of cherry wood, From a small log (5 planks) of perfect wood that I felt it would be sacrilege to cut into short lengths. The sides are each one plank, about 5 cm. thick at the base. Total height 163 cm., width 55 cm., depth 26 cm. Oil finished outside, showcase interior polished. I found the wood in 1968, made the cabinet in 1971.

Left: *Handles on upper doors of the "pagoda" cabinet are of hornbeam, which has the color and texture of ivory.*

Below: *The upper half of the cabinet. Many trials and errors with "practice," or mock-up, doors preceded this solution.*

Details of "pagoda" cabinet. Drawers are of fragrant Lebanon cedar; drawer fronts and pulls of cherry wood. The dovetails are done the way I never tire of doing them.

131

INDEX